Also by Jan Henson Dow

<u>Nonfiction</u>
Writing the Award-Winning Play (with Shannon Michal Dow.)

<u>Poetry</u>
At the Han-ku Pass

<u>Short Plays</u>
Plays that Pop!: One-Act, Ten-Minute, and Monologues

<u>Full-Length Plays</u>
Dark Passages (with Shannon Michal Dow and Robert Schroeder, published by Popular Play Service.)
Dreamers, Shadows, Dreams (with Robert Schroeder, published by Phosphene Publishing Co.)
The Golden Dawn (with Robert Schroeder, published by Phosphene Publishing Co.)
Killing Dante (with Shannon Michal Dow, published by Samuel French, Inc.)
The Magistry (with Robert Schroeder, published by Popular Play Service.)
The Moorlark (with Shannon Michal Dow, published by Phosphene Publishing Co.)
Shaka (with Robert Schroeder, published by Phosphene Publishing Co.)
That Madcap Moon (with Robert Schroeder, published by Phosphene Publishing Co.)

THAT MADCAP MOON

THAT MADCAP MOON

A Play by

Jan Henson Dow
&
Robert Schroeder

Phosphene Publishing Company
Houston, Texas

That Madcap Moon
© 2017 by Jan Henson Dow
ISBN 10: 0-9851477-9-2
ISBN 13: 978-0-9851477-9-2

This play is a work of fiction. Names, characters, places, and incidents either are products of the author's imagination or are used as fiction.

All rights reserved. No part of this work may be copied or otherwise produced or reproduced in any form—printed, electronic, live performance, videotaping, recording, or otherwise—without express permission of Phosphene Publishing Company, except for brief excerpts used in reviews, articles, and critical works.

Published by
Phosphene Publishing Company
Houston, Texas, USA
phosphenepublishing.com

To the memory of my parents:

Celia Bloch Henson
and
Eben Burdet Henson

PRODUCTION OF THAT MADCAP MOON

This edition of *That Madcap Moon* is intended for the reading public only. Theatre professionals and amateurs are hereby informed that the play is subject to production fees. All rights, including professional, amateur, motion pictures, recitation, lecturing, public reading, radio broadcasting, television, and the rights of translation into foreign languages, are strictly reserved.

The amateur live stage performance rights to *That Madcap Moon* are controlled exclusively by Phosphene Publishing Company. There is a fee of $35 to produce this play, and the fee must be paid and rights secured in writing from Phosphene Publishing Company at least two weeks prior to the opening performance of the play. The fee must be paid whether the play is presented for charity or by a nonprofit or profit-seeking organization and whether or not admission is charged.

Professional and stock royalty will be quoted on application to Phosphene Publishing Company.

Copying from this book without express permission of the publisher is strictly forbidden by law, and the right of performance is not transferable.

Whenever the play is produced, the following notice must appear on all programs, printing, and advertising for the play: "Produced by special arrangement with Phosphene Publishing Company."

Due authorship credit must be given on all programs, printing, and advertising for the play.

No one shall commit or authorize any act or omission by which the copyright, or the right to copyright, of this play may be impaired.

No one may make any changes to this play in the process of production, or otherwise.

Correspondence and inquiries may be made through the Phosphene Publishing Company website at phosphenepublishing.com.

THAT MADCAP MOON

CAST OF CHARACTERS
(In order of appearance)

JEFF LOOMIS, a handyman in his 40's or older—eccentric yet warm hearted and reliable.

SARAH ROBINSON, late 40s, a sweet, indomitable woman of misleadingly vague demeanor who runs the Sulphur Spring Inn. Though she is a Jewish woman who grew up in New York City, her speech has taken on the rhythm of the South.

HENRY CLAY WOOD, 11 or 12, a bright and hyperactive boy who lives at the inn with his mother.

JENNY ROBINSON, 14, high-spirited, pretty, and intense—Sarah and Evan Robinson's younger daughter. Her long, brown hair is worn in the style of the period, pulled up on both sides and flowing down her back. She is dressed in a skirt, sweater, saddle shoes, and bobby socks.

MAY ANNE ROBINSON, 18, slim, sweet, direct, and guilelessly attractive—Sarah and Evan's older daughter. She is dressed in a skirt, sweater, loafers and bobby socks.

CPL. TOM YOUNG, 20, handsome in a boyish way—not yet wise in the ways of the world but eagerly purposeful. He has a GI haircut and wears the uniform of a World War II U.S. Army Corporal.

EVAN ROBINSON, late 50's, a hot-tempered, proud Kentuckian of Scots-Irish descent. He is well-dressed in a suit with a vest.

SGT. ALEXANDER KEENE, 39, tall, sensitive, attractive—an exceptionally cosmopolitan American raised in France.

FATHER McGREW, a sincere but naïve Catholic army chaplain in his late 20's or early 30's. He wears a Roman collar and the uniform of a World War II U.S. Army chaplain.

TIME AND PLACE
Early May, 1945—the Sulphur Spring Inn, a guest house in a small town in Kentucky. The inn has only three rooms for rent, but Sarah Robinson has given it a fancier name because she likes the sound of it.

SOUND
Period music is played before the show, during intermission, and at times during the show. There is also the sound of an offstage explosion.

THE SET
The former living room and dining room of a the Robinson family residence—now the lobby and dining room of the Sulphur Spring Inn.

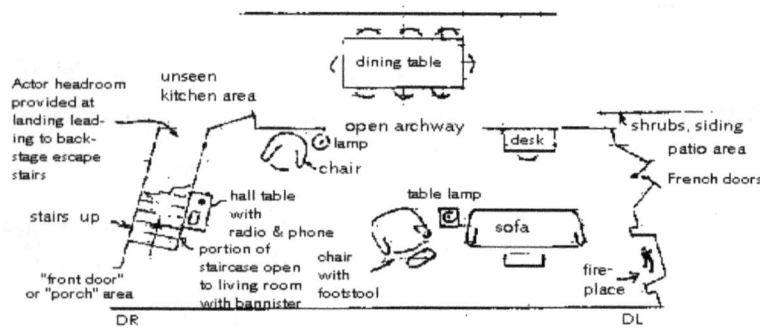

COSTUMING
Period, including World War II U.S. Army uniforms (and, where applicable, GI haircuts).

SCENE SUMMARY
Act One, Scene One: Midafternoon, early May, 1945
Act Two, Scene One: A few minutes later
    Scene Two: An hour later

AUTHORS' NOTES
Sarah Robinson: Sarah is at the emotional center of the play. She is unswerving, warm-hearted, and outgoing. Though she has had little formal education, she is nobody's fool. She should never be played as a "silly" character. Rather, she has her own quirky, kind, and nonjudgmental view of the world and is warmly accepting of the imperfect people in it.

Sarah should never be seen drinking Dr. Snaketoe's Lightnin' Elixir, nor should her unconventional responses ever be played as result of tipsyness. Sarah's offstage intake of her "cure-all" might total only two tablespoons a week. She naïvely believes in the medicinal value of the herbal concoction but remains blithely unaware that the elixir's main attraction is its alcoholic base.

Relationship between Jenny Robinson and Sgt. Keene: There should never be a suggestion of a sexual attraction between Jenny and Sgt. Keene—or that Keene has sexual temptations or intentions regarding Jenny. Rather, they share a spiritual bond, but they both know this cannot overcome the age difference between them. It is therefore important that Jenny is 14 and Keene is 39. This age difference must not be altered—it is essential to the nature of their relationship.

Pacing: This play presents an unusual joining of the comic and the farcical with the innocent, sweet, and wistful. It is essential to the charm and effectiveness of the play that variations in the pacing reflect these alternating modes.

The style and manner of playing must be true to its time: The poignancy and humor of this play derive from character, portrayed 1945 style, and from the rock-solid convictions of the period, so many of which turned out to be temporal.

PROPS

Top of Show Preset

ON COFFEE TABLE
Candy

IN DESK DRAWER
Checkers and checker board

NEAR FIREPLACE DL: Matches

ON TABLE DR
Mail, Phone, and Radio

SARAH
Wedding ring on her finger

ON UL PROP TABLE
JEFF: Firewood
HENRY CLAY: Schoolbooks

ON UR PROP TABLE
SARAH: Feather duster, glass of water, bottle of Elixir, 4 or 5 pots and pans on a string, flowers for dining table
JEFF: Dining room dishes

NEAR UR PROP TABLE
MAY ANNE AND TOM: Rollaway Bed

ON DR PROP TABLE
JENNY: Schoolbooks, Two folded pieces of paper with her poems on them
MAY ANNE: Schoolbooks
EVAN: Bottle of Elixir
JEFF: Twelve boxes of Kotex in traditional blue box

Act Two Scene One Preset

STRIKE
12 boxes of Kotex

ON DR PROP TABLE
EVAN: Small bottle of pills
JENNY: Sack of groceries
HENRY CLAY: Two large cookies

ON UL PROP TABLE
SARAH: Bouquet of flowers
EVAN: 4 or 5 pots and pans on a string

ON UR PROP TABLE
SARAH: Dishes and tableware

Act Two, Scene Two Preset

ON UR PROP TABLE
JEFF: Tray with coffee pot, cups, saucers, cream, sugar
HENRY CLAY: Tray with napkin covering contents, small box
MCGREW: Bottle of Elixir

ON DR PROP TABLE
MCGREW: Several books

THAT MADCAP MOON

ACT I: SCENE ONE

(Period MUSIC should be played during the half hour before curtain time. It is mid-afternoon in early May, 1945. Period MUSIC is coming from the radio on stage. JEFF has entered UL carrying firewood. HE deposits the wood at the fireplace DL and crosses to stand by the radio, listening to the announcer.)

VOICE ON RADIO

Red Army troops have stormed the heart of Berlin, capturing the gutted shell of the German Reichstag and running up the flag of victory.... Following the reports of Adolf Hitler's death, rumors of a German surrender persist. However, President Truman told reporters that no such announcement should be expected today.... Stay tuned for further developments.

(Period MUSIC continues.)

SARAH
(From offstage, UR.)

Jeff! Jeff!

JEFF

I ain't deaf!

(HE pronounces it "deef." He turns the radio off and the MUSIC ceases.)

SARAH
(Entering from the kitchen, UR.)

Jeff, is that you?

(HER slip hangs two inches below the hem of her colorful off-the-rack dress. She wears an apron and a frilly, brightly colored shower cap.)

JEFF
The last time I looked I was me.

SARAH
Jeff, Mister and Miz Stevens will be coming in later tonight. Their son is out at the hospital. So sweep out the back bedroom and get it ready. Oh, and when you finish, go on in and help Aunt Martha mix up another batch of that Elixir. I want to get it bottled before supper.... I think I'll go on out to the spring and get Jenny some of that sulphur water. She's looking kind of peaked.

(SHE pronounces it "peek-ed.")

JEFF
Jenny ain't gonna drink none o' that sulphur water.

SARAH
Well, it would be good for her.

(SARAH exits into the kitchen UR.)

JEFF
(Good-naturedly mocking Sarah.)

Jeff, you jus' pile that wood, 'n' sweep that room, 'n' then in you spare time you go in and stir that Dr. Snaketoe's Lightnin' Elixir with you big toe!

(HENRY CLAY, dressed for school, enters through the French doors, UL, running, carrying his schoolbooks. HE almost collides with JEFF as he crosses—running—throwing his books on the phone stand DR.)

Whoa there, hoss. This ain't no stampede.

HENRY CLAY
Is Jenny home from school yet? There's something important I've got to tell her!

JEFF
I ain't seed her. You Momma is askin' about you.

HENRY CLAY
Momma! Oh, rats! Don't tell her I'm home, Jeff. Tell Jenny I want to see her right away!

(HE runs out the French doors UL. JEFF crosses to the fireplace DL. HE is finishing his preparations at the fireplace as JENNY and MAY ANNE enter at the "front door" DR, carrying school books.)

MAY ANNE
Jeff, did I get any phone calls?

JEFF
I ain't the switchboard.

JENNY
Don't worry. If Tom calls, I'll tell him you're not here.

MAY ANNE
Don't you dare. Jeff, do you know where Mother is?

JEFF

She's out in back thinkin' up somethin' else to keep me busy. That woman scratches when it don't itch.

MAY ANNE

Jeff, why don't you go on out back and ask Mother if I got any phone calls?

JEFF

Cause you leg ain't broke.

JENNY

Jeff, did I get any mail?

JEFF

It's there on the table if you got any. I ain't the Western Union.... Henry Clay is lookin' for you. He say he got somethin' important to tell you.

(JEFF exits into the kitchen, UR.)

MAY ANNE
(Looking through the mail.)
I wonder why Tom hasn't called

JENNY

He's coming for supper. Why should he call?

MAY ANNE

Well, he could at least call.

JENNY

Are you in love with Tom?

MAY ANNE

In love? I don't know. Tom's so handsome in his uniform. And when he rides the bus from the hospital, I'm always afraid it will wreck or something, and he'll never kiss me again. I guess that means I'm in love.

JENNY
Do you think there's more than one way to be in love?

MAY ANNE
What do you mean?

JENNY
Can you be in love with someone's mind?

MAY ANNE
In love with someone's mind? I never thought of that.

JENNY
You know—platonic love—Plato—his theory of the cave?

MAY ANNE
Plato?

JENNY
He was a philosopher back in ancient Greece. He has this theory that what we think is the real world is just an illusion—just shadows.

MAY ANNE
I never thought much about Plato. But I bet I know who you're thinking of!

JENNY
Can't I just ask a simple question?

MAY ANNE
Sgt. Keene is too old for you. You're just a kid.

JENNY
For goodness sake! I didn't say anything about Sgt. Keene! I just asked a philosophical question about Plato!

MAY ANNE
Well, here's a philosophical answer. You know you can have a baby if you fool around when you're not married, don't you?

JENNY
I know that! I'm not ready to have a baby. I wouldn't know what to do with it.

MAY ANNE
Then remember, you're not old enough to be in love and fool around.

JENNY
Do you and Tom fool around?

MAY ANNE
Of course not! I don't call necking "fooling around"!

JENNY
What do you call it?

MAY ANNE
Getting ready to fool around.

JENNY
What does it feel like to be in love?

MAY ANNE
You're always wanting to know what something "feels like."

JENNY
I want to know what everything feels like! I want to go places I've never been, do exciting things I've never done before! I want.... I want....

MAY ANNE
What do you want?

JENNY
Everything! What do you want?

MAY ANNE
I want to get married and have a husband and a house and children and—live happily ever after.

JENNY
Happily ever after? But what then?

MAY ANNE
There is no "what then." That's it.

JENNY
That's it? No it's not! That isn't it! You don't understand! There's got to be something more! Something…something—wonderful!

MAY ANNE
Something wonderful? You're always talking about things I don't understand. I guess I'm not as smart as you are.

JENNY
Yes, you are, May Anne!
    (SHE hugs MAY ANNE)
I don't understand what I'm talking about either.

MAY ANNE
Do you want to try on my silk stockings in a bottle?

JENNY
Silk stockings in a bottle?

MAY ANNE
You rub it on your legs and it looks just like real silk stockings.

JENNY
But the hair on my legs would show through.

MAY ANNE
You should shave your legs. You're old enough for that. And you can have that pair of high heels you're always trying on.

JENNY
High heels! Can I really?

MAY ANNE
We'll fix your hair a different way and try on some lipstick.

JENNY
Okay. I'll be up in a minute.

(MAY ANNE starts up the stairs but pauses when she sees HENRY CLAY, entering by the French doors UL, running.)

HENRY CLAY
Jenny! Jenny!

JENNY
Hey, Henry Clay.

HENRY CLAY
There's something I've got to tell you! I saw…I saw….

MAY ANNE
Henry Clay, do you always have to act like you were shot out of a cannon?

HENRY CLAY
Shhhh! I don't want my mother to know I'm home.

MAY ANNE
Henry Clay, you are the limit!

(SHE exits up the stairs.)

JENNY
What is it, Henry Clay?

HENRY CLAY
I saw them! I saw them together again!

JENNY
Saw who?

HENRY CLAY
That Miz Nelson riding in a car with your father, just like last week.

JENNY
So what? That doesn't mean anything. She's my mother's friend. My mother helped find her a job when she first came to town.

HENRY CLAY
Well, she's your father's girlfriend now. I saw them!

JENNY
You don't know anything, Henry Clay. You're too young to know anything.

HENRY CLAY
Yes, I do, too! My father had a girlfriend before he went overseas. I saw them together. They were kissing. That's why my mother's—the way she is.

JENNY
Well, you don't know anything about my father! Anyhow, don't tell my mother what you saw. Promise?

HENRY CLAY
Okay. I promise. I never tell my mother anything.

(CPL. TOM YOUNG enters DR.)

TOM
Jenny! Jenny!

HENRY CLAY
Tom, did you shoot targets yet? Did you win any sharpshooter medals?

TOM
Shhhh, Henry Clay. If I win any medals, I'll give them all to you.... Jenny, where is May Anne?

JENNY
Upstairs. She wasn't expecting you 'til supper.

TOM
I've got to see her! Now!

JENNY
I'll call her. May Anne! May Anne!!

TOM
Shhhh!

JENNY
What do you mean, shhhh? You told me you wanted to see May Anne!

TOM
I do! But not anybody else!

HENRY CLAY
Are you on the lam? Did you kill your commanding officer, like you always said you would?

MAY ANNE
(Entering from upstairs.)
Did you call? ... Tom!
(MAY ANNE hurries into TOM'S arms.)
You're so early!

TOM
We have to talk!

MAY ANNE
Jenny, would you mind?

JENNY
Not in the least. Go ahead and talk.

MAY ANNE
Tom and I would like a little privacy, Jenny! Henry Clay!

JENNY
Well, pardon me! If you can find any privacy in this house, you can have it!

(JENNY and HENRY CLAY retreat to the hall DR where they stand listening, HENRY CLAY mimicking TOM'S actions. TOM and MAY ANNE cross to the fireplace DL.)

MAY ANNE
Tom, what is it?

TOM
They've just posted the list. The next shipment to Indiantown Gap. I'm on it. I'm headed overseas!

MAY ANNE
Oh, no! ... Tom!

(TOM and MAY ANNE hug again.)

HENRY CLAY
(Putting his hands to his breast in an exaggerated manner.)
"Oh, no! . . . Tom!"

JENNY
(To HENRY CLAY as SHE tries to keep from laughing.)
Shhhh!

TOM
We get a three-day pass. I'm on it now!

MAY ANNE
Three days! And then you....

TOM
Don't think about that! Think about the three days!

MAY ANNE
But you'll be going....

TOM
With you! To a preacher! To a justice of the peace!

MAY ANNE
Tom! You're out of your mind!

HENRY CLAY
"Tom, you're out of your mind!"

TOM
May Anne, I want us to get married before I go!

JENNY and HENRY CLAY
Married?!

MAY ANNE
Married? We're not even engaged! I don't even have a ring!

TOM
There isn't time for a ring! I only have a three-day pass!
    (HE draws HER back into his arms.)
We'll get married right away! May Anne! Three days! Three nights! Together!

HENRY CLAY
    (Again acting in an exaggerated manner, falling on one knee and taking JENNY'S hand.)
"Oh, darling, three days, three nights, together!"

    (HENRY CLAY clutches his throat and falls to the floor.)

JENNY
Shhhh!

MAY ANNE
Henry Clay, get up from that floor! You are acting like a fool!
    (To TOM.)
I don't know what to say. Oh, no! What would my father say?

JENNY
I could tell you what he'd say.

MAY ANNE
Would you just stay out of this, Miss Nosy Parker!
    (To TOM.)
We can't talk here. There's no privacy.

TOM

We have to talk. Where can we go?

MAY ANNE

We'll go upstairs. Jenny, don't tell Momma Tom is here. Henry Clay, don't you say a word!

JENNY

You mean don't tell Momma that Tom is in your bedroom? I can understand that.

HENRY CLAY

Even I can understand that!

MAY ANNE

Just keep Momma downstairs, whatever you have to do. Please!

>   (TOM and MAY ANNE cross to the stairs and start up the steps.)

JENNY

You know Momma. You can't keep her down anywhere. Oh, all right! Go on.... Why am I always in the middle of everything?

JEFF
>   (Entering from kitchen UR, seeing MAY ANNE and TOM.)

You better not let you Momma see Tom goin' up those stairs!

MAY ANNE

It's all right, Jeff. We're just going to talk.

>   (MAY ANNE and TOM exit up the stairs. JEFF sits on the sofa.)

JEFF

I bet you do.

JENNY

Jeff, where is Momma?

JEFF

You Momma went out to the spring to get a jug of that sulphur water. She went to get it specially for you. She say you lookin' kinda peaked.

JENNY

Ugh-gh! That sulphur water! I'll tell her you're looking peaked and she'll make you drink it.

JEFF

She's been tryin' long's I've known her to make me drink that pee-ew-ey water. Ain't got it done yet.

JENNY

We'll make Henry Clay drink it!

HENRY CLAY

Oh, no, you won't!

SARAH
(From offstage UR.)

Jenny, is that you?

JEFF

Here she come. If she ask where I am, tell her....

(HE starts to exit but is stopped by SARAH, who enters from the kitchen UR with a large feather duster under her arm, carrying a glass of sulphur water and a bottle of Elixir.)

SARAH

Jeff, where are you going?

JEFF

I'm on my way to Memphis.

SARAH

(Putting the water glass and the bottle on the radio and handing JEFF the duster.)

Here, before you go, I want you to give this room a good dusting.

JEFF

I done dusted this room last week. Don't need no more dustin'.

SARAH

(Running HER finger over the furniture and holding the finger up.)

What do you call this?

JEFF

Looks like a mighty dusty finger.

(JEFF begins to dust with a feeble up-and-down motion.)

SARAH

(Kissing JENNY.)

How was school today?

JENNY

(Brightly.)

It was boring.

SARAH

(Absentmindedly.)

That's nice. Jenny, don't go off anywhere before supper. Your father is coming by on his way home from the doctor. He'll want to see you.

JENNY
Well, I don't want to see him.

SARAH
You shouldn't talk like that. Why, Henry Clay will think you don't like your own father.

HENRY CLAY
I saw Mr. Robinson! He was driving in a car—with that....

JENNY
Henry Clay! Never mind! Momma, you just don't understand. Daddy doesn't care a thing about us.... He doesn't like it that you're Jewish and don't come from an old Kentucky family like he does.

SARAH
Why, you come from the same family. You're Scotch-Irish like your father's people. You're just like your father.

JENNY
I'm not a thing like Daddy! I'm half Jewish and half Scotch-Irish and nobody will let me be what I am!

SARAH
You can be whatever you want to be.

JENNY
No, I can't! Here in Kentucky I have to be Scotch-Irish and forget I'm Jewish, and when we go to visit Aunt Eva in New York, they want me to be Jewish and forget I'm Scotch-Irish!

SARAH
Aunt Eva never says anything about what you are.

JENNY

No, but that funny little old woman who comes to visit Aunt Eva always calls me "that little shiksa" under her breath.

HENRY CLAY

What's a "little shiksa"?

SARAH

People say all kinds of things. It's what they do that counts. Your father loves you very much.

JENNY

Well, he has a strange way of showing it. He doesn't even live here anymore! He lives out at the farm! It's so embarrassing! Why doesn't he just stay out there?

HENRY CLAY

My father went off with someone else. He's not coming back.

SARAH

But he's still your father, and you still love him.

JENNY

Momma, don't tell us how we're supposed to feel!

SARAH

You'll understand when you're older.

JENNY

I don't see Daddy understanding—and he's older.

SARAH

Your father loves you very much. Henry Clay, you better go on upstairs. Your mother was asking about you. Go on now.

HENRY CLAY
Oh, rats!

  (HE exits upstairs.)

SARAH
I'd better check that back bedroom myself.
  (SHE crosses toward the stairs.)
Is May Anne home yet?

  (JENNY hurriedly crosses to a position between SARAH and the stairs.)

JENNY
(Blocking SARAH'S path.)
May Anne?

SARAH
Your sister—May Anne.

JENNY
Oh, that May Anne.

SARAH
She's usually home by now. I wonder what she's doing?

JENNY
I'm not sure—exactly—what she's doing.

SARAH
I wonder if Tom is still coming for supper?

JENNY
Tom?

SARAH

May Anne's Tom.

JENNY

Oh, that Tom. I'd expect to see him any minute, if I were you.
(SARAH again heads for the stairs, but JENNY pulls her into the living room.)
Mother, what in the world do you have on your head?

SARAH

Oh, this? It's just a shower cap Miz Clifford gave me.

JENNY

Well, it looks terrible! Don't let Daddy see you in that shower cap!

SARAH

It was nice of her to give it to me, so I thought I should wear it.

JEFF

Miz Robinson, this feather duster don't do no good. Makes that dust just fly up in the air and set right back down in the same place.

(HE flicks the duster up and down, then SARAH takes the duster from him.)

SARAH

No, do it like this, Jeff.
(SHE vigorously dusts sideways.)
Instead of like this.
(SHE vigorously dusts up and down.)
Let that dust set someplace else for a change.
(SHE hands the duster back to JEFF.)

JEFF

Miz Robinson, that don't make no sense.

SARAH
I know, Jeff. That's the trouble with dusting. There's no sense to it. It's the thought that counts.

>(SARAH starts for the stairs. Seeking to keep HER from going upstairs, JEFF grabs the glass of water from the radio.)

JEFF
Miz Robinson, did you get this here sulphur water for Jenny?

SARAH
>(Taking the glass from JEFF.)

Oh, that's right. I forgot.
>(SARAH tries to hand the glass to JENNY.)

Here, I told Jeff you're looking peaked. Are you anemic? Drink this sulphur water. It's good for you.

JENNY
>(Pushing the glass away.)

Momma, I don't want it! Make Jeff drink it.

SARAH
Jeff likes it. Don't you, Jeff?

JEFF
Pee-ew-ey!

JENNY
It stinks and it tastes terrible.

JEFF
It shor do.

>(HE resumes his unenthusiastic dusting.)

SARAH

It's got to taste terrible to do any good. Why, rich people pay good money to go to a sulphur spring, and we've got one right on our own place, the Sulphur Spring Inn.

JENNY

A fancy name for three extra bedrooms that we rent out. I don't call that an Inn!

SARAH

Why, people come here just for the water.

JENNY

They come here, Momma, because there's a mental hospital over at Darnell for the soldiers, and their families come to see them, and there isn't a room in town that isn't full. You're the only one I know around here who drinks that water.

SARAH

Well, yes, that's true. But this sulphur water is just what those people need. A little spring tonic never hurt anybody. It flushes out the system.

JENNY

Well, I don't want my system flushed out! And take that awful shower cap off before Daddy sees you!

SARAH

(Setting down the glass and noticing the bottle of Elixir.)

Just a little gift.

(SARAH removes the shower cap and puts it in her apron pocket then picks up the bottle.)

Miz Clifford wants this Elixir. Why don't you take it on over?

JENNY
Momma, you know what Daddy said about you selling that quack medicine.

SARAH
Why, everyone—Miz Clifford and Miz Waldrop—they all say it's done them a world of good.

JENNY
Mother, if Daddy finds out you're still making that stuff—well, just don't get me in on it, that's all. Leave me out of it.

SARAH
Well, what he doesn't know won't hurt him.

JENNY
Momma, he thinks what you don't know won't hurt you!

SARAH
And he's right. Here, take this bottle on over to Miz Clifford.

JENNY
Jeff can take it.

JEFF
No, I cain't. I got to move this dust from over here to over there.

JENNY
Mother, I worked hard at school all day. Can't I have a little rest and relaxation?

SARAH
Oh, all right. I'll get May Anne to do it. May Anne!
>(Again SARAH starts toward the stairs. HENRY CLAY enters, running down the stairs.)

Henry Clay, have you seen May Anne?

HENRY CLAY
Yes, ma'am.

JENNY
Henry Clay!

HENRY CLAY
I've seen her—lots of times.

JENNY
(HER mind racing to think of another deterrent to Sarah's going upstairs.)
Momma, wait a minute! Your slip is showing again!

SARAH
Oh, yes. I meant to pin it up. What did I do with that pin?
(SARAH puts the bottle on the hall table.)

JENNY
Here it is.
(JENNY unpins the safety pin from SARAH'S collar then reaches down inside the front of SARAH'S dress, pinning up the slip. As she does, she calls upstairs loudly.)
Momma's slip is showing and I'm pinning it up!

JEFF
(Also calling upstairs loudly.)
You Momma has come all unpinned!

SARAH
(Puzzled, but in a sweet voice.)
Sometimes I think we are all going nuts.

JENNY
(Finishing pinning up the slip.)
Sometimes I think so, too. There, that's better.

SARAH

Next thing you know, they'll put all of us out at Darnell Hospital.

JENNY

I wouldn't be surprised.

HENRY CLAY

Me either.

SARAH

Jeff, have you seen May Anne?

JEFF

Yes, ma'am.

JENNY

Jeff!

JEFF

I've seen her lots of times. You lookin' for her? I'll go see if I can find her.

(Joyfully discarding the feather duster, HE exits thru the French doors UL.)

SARAH
(To JENNY.)

Why don't you go on now and take that Elixir to Miz Clifford?

JENNY

Mother, she's so gloomy.

SARAH

I know. Ever since her only son was killed overseas, she just stays inside, grieving. She needs to see people, get out of herself. A little visit makes her feel so much better.

JENNY
I'm not very good at making people feel better.

SARAH
It just takes a little practice. Oh, never mind. I'll get May Anne to take it over. Where is she?
        (SARAH crosses to the stairs.)
May Anne!

JENNY
        (Hurriedly crossing to the stairs and calling loudly.)
Momma wants me to go on and take this Elixir to Miz Clifford, so don't blame me!

        (JENNY takes the bottle from the hall table.)

HENRY CLAY
I'll go with you.

JENNY
Here I am again—in the middle of everything!

HENRY CLAY
        (Happily.)
Me, too!

        (JENNY and HENRY CLAY exit DR.)

SARAH
        (Calling after them.)
You and Henry Clay come right back. Your father will want to see you! Sometimes I don't know what gets into that child.
        (Calling upstairs.)
May Anne! Are you home?

MAY ANNE
(Entering from upstairs.)

Momma, I heard you. I was just coming down. There's something I have to tell you. Come in here where no one can hear us.

> (MAY ANNE leads SARAH DC, so that SARAH can't see TOM entering, running down the stairs, carrying his shoes. TOM hurries out the "front door" DR, then, on the "porch," puts his shoes on—tries to tie the laces but fumbles and fails—then re-enters the hallway, as if he has just arrived at the house.)

SARAH
Who's going to hear us?

MAY ANNE
Momma, in this house you never know.

SARAH
Jenny is acting awfully strange, and so are you. Well, what did you want to tell me?

MAY ANNE
Well, it's about Tom and me....
> (As if seeing TOM for the first time today.)

Oh, look! Tom is here!

SARAH
Why, Tom, where did you come from? We weren't expecting you 'til supper.

TOM
How are you, Miz Robinson?

SARAH
Why, I'm fit as a fiddle.

TOM

Yes, ma'am, you sure are.

MAY ANNE

Momma, Tom and I have something important we want to talk to you about.

SARAH

The way you all are acting, I'm afraid to ask what it is.

MAY ANNE

It's nothing—unusual. People do it every day.

SARAH

I bet they do. Now what is it?

MAY ANNE

Momma, Tom and I want to get married.

SARAH

Married…!

MAY ANNE

Right away because he's going to be sent overseas any day, but if we do get married, we'll have to live here with you because all the rooms in town are taken, and we don't have any money for an apartment because we only have forty-two dollars in quarters we saved in my piggy bank.

SARAH

Oh, brother! Is that all?

MAY ANNE

And we want you to help tell Daddy, and convince him it's all right.

TOM
We thought maybe you could sell him on the idea.

SARAH
(Almost to herself.)
Oh, brother!

MAY ANNE
Oh, Momma, please help us.

SARAH
May Anne, you know what your father will say.

MAY ANNE
Oh, Momma, I know what he'll say. "May Anne, you're only eighteen! You're too young to get married! You're too young to go out with soldiers! You're too young to do anything!"

SARAH
That's not all he'll say.

MAY ANNE
Oh, Momma, I don't think Daddy even believes in marriage!

SARAH
He believes in it all right—the way he believes in death and taxes.

MAY ANNE
I don't think Daddy was ever young.

SARAH
Well, not recently.

MAY ANNE
He never wants me to do anything.

SARAH
Getting married on forty-two dollars in your piggy bank would be one of those things.

TOM
I love May Anne very much, Miz Robinson.

SARAH
I know you do, Tom. But you're both so young! Mr. Robinson wants May Anne and Jenny to graduate from college and have a career—not be stuck in this backwater town like he was.

MAY ANNE
Jenny'll have the career. She's just like him. Both stubborn as mules! Oh, Momma, please help us! I'll just die if Tom is sent overseas and we aren't married! I'll just die if they send him into battle! Think of it—into the front lines!

TOM
The front lines!

SARAH
Kentucky is not exactly the front lines, so Tom is safe for the moment.

MAY ANNE
Oh, Momma!

SARAH
Now, just slow down. Let's think about this.... Don't say a word to your father, for now. Tom, you go on back to the hospital tonight, and we'll all sleep on it.

TOM
Go back to the hospital?

MAY ANNE
But Tom can't go back to the hospital.

SARAH
Why, of course he can.

(TOM signals frantically to MAY ANNE, emphatically shaking his head "no.")

MAY ANNE
No, he can't. He got a three-day pass, and if he goes back, that mean ole Sgt. Myers will think up something to keep him there. We may never see each other again.

TOM
Never see each other again!

SARAH
But where in the world is he going to stay? Every room in town is full.
(Reading MAY ANNE'S mind.)
Oh, no!

MAY ANNE
Momma, why can't he stay here?

SARAH
Now, May Anne, if your father found out Tom stayed here overnight, he'd have a conniption fit for sure.

MAY ANNE
Momma, if you won't let Tom stay here, I'll just pack my bag and my piggy bank and we'll just—elope!

SARAH
Elope? Where to? There isn't an empty room in town.

MAY ANNE
We'll—just go out into the night—with my piggy bank—wandering from door to door....

SARAH
You'll do no such thing!
> (Pause, thinking.)

Well, there is a roll-away bed back there somewhere. Tom could use that.

MAY ANNE
Oh, Momma!

SARAH
I know! We could put the roll-away bed in Sgt. Keene's room and Tom can spend the night there. Sgt. Keene won't mind.

TOM
I'm to spend the night in Sgt. Keene's room?

SARAH
Yes, and he can keep an eye on you. Won't that be nice?

TOM
Yes, ma'am, but I thought....

SARAH
I know what you thought, Tom. We'll have a nice talk after supper.

MAY ANNE
Mother! After supper?

SARAH
Well, we've all got to eat sometime. Now, you and Tom go on and find that roll-away bed. I think it's back there in the storeroom.

(SARAH exits into the kitchen UR.)

MAY ANNE
(Crossing toward UR.)
Come on.

TOM
A roll-away bed? In Sgt. Keene's room? May Anne!

MAY ANNE
At least you'll be here and not out there! And maybe....

TOM
Oh! May Anne!

MAY ANNE
The bed's out here.

(MAY ANNE exits into the kitchen UR, TOM following. SARAH enters through the dining room UC, followed by JEFF. SARAH is carrying four or five pots and pans hanging from a string.)

SARAH
Here, take these pots and pans and hang them on the side porch.

(The pots and pans clang against each other, making a loud clatter as SARAH hands them to JEFF. HE holds them before him, staring at them in amazement.)

JEFF
Hang them? On the side porch?

SARAH
So they won't disturb Mr. Robinson.

JEFF
I seen him in a fit 'bout lots of things but never 'bout no pots and pans.

SARAH
Jeff, that sweet young thing who just moved in up the street—her husband's a patient out at the hospital. She hardly has any money. I'm finding her a job.

JEFF
Selling these here pots and pans? They ain't no money in it.

SARAH
No, Jeff, she doesn't have any pots and pans to cook in. They're so hard to get. It's the war, I guess. I told her she could stop by and pick these up from the side porch.

JEFF
If Mr. Robinson finds out you givin' away these here pots and pans....

SARAH
Now, Jeff, they're just on loan.

JEFF
On loan? Like that handsaw and them pliers and them clippin' shears o' his you done give away last fall? And now it's pots and pans! Look out!

(JEFF exits at the French doors UL with the pots and pans. Excitedly, running, JENNY and HENRY CLAY enter at the "front door" DR. JENNY is still carrying the Elixir.)

JENNY
Momma! Momma!

SARAH

Oh, brother. What now?

JENNY

Daddy's Buick just turned the corner....

HENRY CLAY

...headed this way!

SARAH

Oh, no! If he sees Tom, we'll have the war right here in our own living room! May Anne! Tom!

JENNY

What do you want me to do with this Elixir?

SARAH

I told you to take it on over to Miz Clifford!

JENNY

I couldn't. She won't answer the door. Here, I don't want it!

(JENNY hands the bottle to SARAH.)

SARAH

Well, here....
(SARAH passes the bottle to HENRY CLAY.)
Hide it! Anything! But don't let Mr. Robinson see it!

(Handling the bottle like a hot potato, HENRY CLAY quickly flips it to JENNY.)

JENNY

Oh, no you don't!
(JENNY slaps the bottle into SARAH'S hand.)
You hide it from Daddy. You've had more practice than I have.

(MAY ANNE and TOM enter from the kitchen UR, pushing the roll-away bed.)

SARAH

Oh, no! Don't bring that bed in here!

(SARAH quickly slips the bottle behind a sofa pillow.)

MAY ANNE

But Mother, you told us....

SARAH

Your father's Buick just turned the corner, and he's headed this way!

MAY ANNE and TOM

Headed this way!

(TOM and MAY ANNE panic. TOM flees to the kitchen, as MAY ANNE wrestles the bed. TOM returns, and HENRY CLAY rushes to help. The three push and pull the bed, each having a different idea as to what to do with it.)

SARAH

Wait a minute! I know! Tom, now slow down. Just walk out the front door as if nothing had happened.

TOM

The front door!

SARAH

Speak politely if you're spoken to. Just say, "Good afternoon." But don't stop and talk, whatever you do!

(SARAH shoves TOM to the "doorway" DR. Reluctantly, TOM exits.)

MAY ANNE

Oh, mother! You're not sending Tom away?

SARAH

Now, don't start wailing. We're just testing the waters. Let's see how your father reacts to a simple "Good afternoon" before we start talking about marriage.... May Anne, you and Henry Clay shove that bed out the side door.... And stay out there! Your father can read your face like a book, and it's got trouble written all over it.

MAY ANNE

Momma!

SARAH

Now go on!
(JENNY crosses to the stairs.)
Jenny, where are you going?

JENNY

I know what's coming: the Sulphur Spring Civil War, and I'm not going to get caught in the middle of it!

(JENNY exits up the stairs. Awkwardly, MAY ANNE and HENRY CLAY push the bed toward the French doors UL. THEY are maneuvering the bed over the door sill as EVAN, carrying a bottle, enters at the "front door" DR.)

EVAN

Sarah!

SARAH

Evan, is that you?

EVAN

Who else would be speaking in my voice? May Anne, where are you going with that bed?

MAY ANNE
(In wide-eyed innocence.)
Where am I going? I don't know.

(MAY ANNE and HENRY CLAY quickly exit with the bed UL.)

EVAN

Sarah, where is she going with that bed?

SARAH
(In wide-eyed innocence.)
Where is she going? I don't know.

EVAN

Who was that soldier coming out this door like he was a shot out of a cannon?

SARAH

Who was who?

EVAN

Don't bat your eyes at me. You know who! That soldier blasting out this front door!

SARAH

Oh, that soldier! Why, he's just a very nice young man stationed out at the hospital.

EVAN

To you they're all "nice young men." If I asked you who was Jesse James, "Why, he's just a nice young man who got blamed for robbing some banks." I've told you and told you: I don't want any of those Section Eight soldiers hanging around here!

SARAH

Now, Evan, don't get your blood pressure up. You know what the doctor says.

EVAN

I don't give a damn what that doctor says! He doesn't know his ass from his elbow! I didn't come here to talk about that doctor!

SARAH

Whatever is the matter now?

EVAN

I ask you, what is this?

(HE holds high the bottle he is carrying.)

SARAH

Why, it looks like a bottle.

EVAN

You know damn good and well what it is! It's a bottle of that Dr. Snaketoe's Lightnin' Elixir that I told you to stop peddling!

SARAH

Why, it is, isn't it? Imagine that. Wherever did you get it?

EVAN

"Wherever did you get it?" Don't play cat and mouse with me! I know you too well! I know you through and through! I'm campaigning up some god-forsaken back road. This old codger comes out of a cabin half falling down in the ditch—looks like he doesn't have a pot to piss in. When I tell him I sure would appreciate his vote, what does he say?

SARAH

I don't know. What does he say?

EVAN

"Are you the husband of that sweet-faced little woman who runs the inn? Well, tell her I'm goin' to come into town and get me another bottle of her Elixir. It done me a world of good," he says. "And if you're her husband, you sure got my vote!" And he gives me this empty bottle.

SARAH

Well, wasn't that nice of him!

EVAN

Nice? God Almighty, Sarah! I am trying to run for congress! With your schemes they wouldn't elect me dog catcher!

SARAH

I didn't know you were running for dog catcher, too.

EVAN

You know damn good and well I'm running for congress! I've told you and told you—I don't want you selling this quack medicine!
  (HE waves the bottle in HER face.)
Dr. Snaketoe's Lightnin' Elixir! I won't be made a laughing stock around here!

SARAH

That Joe McGinnis told me himself it's an old Indian remedy.

EVAN

Indian remedy my eye! That four-flusher Joe McGinnis! When he traded you that recipe, he knew damn good and well it wasn't worth the powder to blow him to hell!

SARAH

Why, a lot of people swear by that Elixir. It's done them a world of good.

EVAN

Now, I won't tell you again! I won't have you hawking this trash all around town! I stopped you from bottling that sulphur water! Now it's Dr. Snaketoe's Lightnin' Elixir! Next thing I know, you'll be selling stock in a gold mine you found in the backyard—and they'll buy it!

SARAH

Is there gold back there? I didn't know that.

EVAN

Sarah! Why is it every time I try to put some sense into your head, what comes out is nonsense?

SARAH

I don't know. It just comes over me, and I say the first thing that pops into my head. I wonder why I do that?

EVAN

Sarah, now try to listen to me. You know how much I want to be elected to congress!

SARAH

I know—so you can straighten everybody out—including me.

EVAN

If I could straighten you out, that would be up there with paying off the national debt! Sarah, what a congressman needs is a proper wife—one who can give little teas and preside over social functions in Washington society.

SARAH

A proper wife? Like Lucille?

EVAN

Leave Lucille out of this! I am not talking about Lucille!

SARAH

We never talk about Lucille.

EVAN

She is just a friend.

SARAH

(Wistfully.)
I know all about what kind of friend. She and I were friends—once. Maybe she would like to move to Washington.

EVAN

Lucille is not moving to Washington! And I can just see you in Washington—bottling equal parts of Snaketoe's Elixir and sulphur water and peddling it to visiting heads of state!

SARAH

Aunt Martha and I would certainly have to buy more bottles. Those people in Washington probably all need their systems flushed out.

EVAN

Sarah!

SARAH

I guess it's the war.

EVAN

God Almighty, Sarah! You can't blame congress's constipation on the war! Blame man's insufferable greed and his damned stupidity! That's what I intend to do something about when I get elected—clean out all the riffraff in government.

SARAH

I don't think I have enough bottles for that!

EVAN

Sarah!

SARAH

Now, Evan, you know you can rely on me. Especially if Lucille takes off with that lieutenant colonel she's been seen with around town.

EVAN

She has not been "seen with" any lieutenant colonel. They are just friends.

SARAH

The whole town knows what kind of friends.

EVAN

Sarah! That is a vicious rumor—vile! And I never expected to hear that from you! I am shocked! Deeply shocked!

SARAH

I know, it is vile—even if it is true.

EVAN

Sarah, your mind just keeps flitting from here to there. The trouble with you is, you do not have an educated mind.

SARAH

I know. You should have married someone who has an education—someone who quit college when you did.

EVAN

I did not quit college! I had to leave—to help support the family. That's why I want Jenny and May Anne to go to college and make something of themselves. I don't want them to have no education and no career, like you, for instance, and have to settle for marriage.

SARAH

To someone like you, for instance.

EVAN

Not someone like me, damn it!

SARAH

But someone like Lucille—who has an education—seems to prefer lieutenant colonels.

EVAN

Lucille does not prefer Lieutenant Colonels! We are not talking about Lucille! You keep Lucille out of this!

SARAH

I would be glad to keep Lucille out of—all of this!

EVAN

Sarah—you have had every chance in the world to... to....

SARAH

I know. I am sorry, Evan. I am not the wife you always wanted.

EVAN

Sarah, you—exasperate me! And so do—soldiers!
> (Aware of HIS slip as to his real feelings and quickly attempting to cover it over.)

I mean—those soldiers hanging around May Anne! That one who came flying out this front door! What does May Anne know about that soldier? Where is May Anne?

SARAH

May Anne? Did you say, "Where is May Anne?"

EVAN
We do have a daughter named May Anne, don't we? The one who vanished out the side door pushing a bed.

SARAH
Oh, that May Anne.
> (Calling out the side door.)

May Anne!

> (MAY ANNE does not immediately respond.)

EVAN
Where's Jenny?

SARAH
Jenny?

EVAN
Good God! Are you going deaf?

SARAH
Sometimes I think I am. I'll call her. Jenny! Jenny, come here…. Where did she get to?

EVAN
She always makes herself scarce when I come by. What's the matter with that child?

SARAH
She's just young. The young don't understand. They're too set in their ways.

EVAN
I thought that was reserved for the old. Jenny! Jenny!

JENNY
(Slowly entering from upstairs.)

I'm coming.

EVAN
Come here. Let me look at you. Sarah, doesn't this child ever eat anything? She's as thin as a rail.

SARAH
I know. She doesn't eat a thing. Just a bite here and a bite there. I try to get her to drink the waters.

EVAN
Well, what can you expect? Raising her with this riffraff you've got around here!

JENNY
Daddy! When families visit soldiers who are wounded, that doesn't make them riffraff!

EVAN
Wounded, my eye! Most of them are bucking for a Section Eight discharge! Anything to stay out of the fighting! A soldier with any guts wouldn't be goofing off in that damned mental hospital!

SARAH
Now, Evan, it's not the poor boys' fault. It's the war!

EVAN
God Almighty, Sarah, you can't blame riffraff on the war! My only son is God knows where. That you can blame on the war.

SARAH
The last letter I got from Andrew was almost a month ago. I'm worried about him. He may be in the war this very minute.

JENNY

If the war is at the University of Chicago, he's sure in it. Mother, we know where Andrew is. He just became an ensign at Officer Candidate School. He's in Chicago!

EVAN

That's what that Roosevelt gang wants you to believe. They've probably already sent him to the Pacific.

JENNY

But his letters come from the University of Chicago!

EVAN

The University of Chicago—that den of New Dealers and Communists!

JENNY

Daddy! You just won't listen!

EVAN

Why is it that you and May Anne never listen to a thing I say?

SARAH

They're just young, Evan. You're only young once.

EVAN

Thank God! Once is enough for anyone. Speaking of being young....
    (Calling.)
May Anne! My God! She's out there with that bed! Where's that soldier?
    (Crossing to the French doors and shouting furiously.)
May Anne! So there you are! Come in here!
    (MAY ANNE enters from French doors UL.)
Have you seen that soldier I saw tearing out of this house?

MAY ANNE

What soldier?

EVAN

The one doing the hundred yard dash down the front walk.

MAY ANNE

Oh, that soldier. Daddy, his name is Tom Young, and he's a very nice young man.

JENNY

From a very nice family.

EVAN

How many times have I heard that one? You and your mother haven't got the brains God gave a goose when it comes to men—and I should know!

MAY ANNE

Daddy, if you'd just listen....

EVAN

Now you listen! I don't want you going out with any of those so-called soldiers from out at that slacker's hospital! And I don't want them hanging around this house!

MAY ANNE

But Daddy! I've got to go out with somebody!

EVAN

There are plenty of boys over at the college you can go out with! They're not worth the paper to type their draft deferments, but that's another story.

MAY ANNE

Oh, Daddy, there aren't any boys over at the college I'd be seen dead with. All the ones left have flat feet or hernias or something, and I'm not going to go out with them.

EVAN
Good! You don't need to go out with anyone.

MAY ANNE
Daddy! I'm eighteen years old! If I never have any dates, I'll never get married! I'll be an old maid!

EVAN
You have your whole life ahead of you to make all kinds of mistakes—like marriage, for instance—but not under this roof!

MAY ANNE
Oh, Daddy!

> (MAY ANNE bursts into tears and runs upstairs. At the French doors UL, TOM peeks in. SARAH sees him, and motions him away. TOM exits.)

JENNY
Daddy! If you would just listen!

EVAN
The women in this house should listen! I'll stop by later with some extra ration coupons.
   (Heading for the French doors UL.)
Are those pruning shears Jeff borrowed on the porch? I'd better take them along before you give them away to the first person you see.

JENNY
   (Trying to block HIS path.)
Oh, Daddy! I'll get them!

SARAH

(Also hurriedly trying to block EVAN'S path, almost colliding with JENNY.)

Oh, no! Don't bother! I'll get them!

EVAN

Never mind. I'll just go out that way.

(Sidestepping SARAH and JENNY, EVAN crosses to the French doors UL. There is the SOUND of a loud clatter. EVAN sees TOM.)

Young man, come in here!

(TOM enters with the pots and pans hanging around his neck.)

What are you doing with these pots and pans?

TOM

(In a panic.)

I don't know!

SARAH

Now Evan, don't get all excited. They're just a few pots and pans.

EVAN

Just a few pots and pans! Young man, who are you?

TOM

(Immediately snapping to the rigid military stance of "Attention," TOM rattles his response as he has been trained to do—loudly and distinctly.)

Corporal Thomas Young! Sir! 35555025!

EVAN

What are you doing, skulking out there? Do you want to get arrested for trespassing, and stealing our pots and pans?

TOM
No, sir! I mean, well, sir, it's like this. I was waiting to speak to you, sir!

EVAN
Waiting. That's why you were doing the hundred yard dash down the front walk?

TOM
(Continuing to stand rigidly at "Attention.")
Yes, sir! I mean, no, sir! It's like this, sir! There's something important I want to say to you, sir!

> (TOM has emphasized each repetition of the word "sir.")

SARAH
Yes, there's something important he wants to say.

EVAN
Well, say it!

TOM
I— ah....

SARAH
Start with, "Good afternoon," Tom.

TOM
Good afternoon, Tom.

SARAH
Relax now, Tom. And just go on....

TOM
(Relaxing from the position of "Attention.")
I, ah, well, ah, it's like this....

EVAN

Young man, speak up! Are you afraid of me?

TOM

Yes, sir! I mean, no, sir!

EVAN

Well, you should be! I don't know you, and I don't want to know you. Is that clear?

TOM

Yes, sir!

SARAH

Now, Evan, Tom is a very nice young man.

EVAN

Then you tell this very nice young man to go out that very nice front door, down that very nice front walk, and don't ever let me see his face in this house again!

TOM

Yes, sir!

(TOM takes off pots and pans, hands them to SARAH, and crosses rapidly to the "front door" DR.)

EVAN

(To TOM.)

Is that clear?

TOM

Yes, sir!

(TOM exits.)

EVAN
(To SARAH.)
Is that clear?

SARAH
But, Evan, there's something you should know.

EVAN
There's a lot I'd like to know! Let's start with these pots and pans!

SARAH
(As SHE forcefully tosses the strung-together pots and pans out the French doors UL, then shouts over the clatter.)
What pots and pans?

JEFF
(Entering from the kitchen UR.)
Miz Robinson, do you want us to start bottling that Elixir now, or wait 'til it cools?
(Noticing EVAN.)
Oh, oh! 'Scuse me!
(Performing an elaborate about-face, JEFF exits rapidly UR.)

EVAN
Sarah.

SARAH
Now, Evan, I'll get rid of it. You know you can count on me.

EVAN
I can count on you to be the death of me!

(HE exits through the French doors UL.)

HENRY CLAY
(Running in DR.)
Can I come back in now? Did I miss anything?

JENNY
How can you stand Daddy when he's like that? Why don't you just get a divorce? Then maybe he won't come around here anymore.

SARAH
We've been married a long time.
(SARAH puts her arm around HENRY CLAY'S shoulders.)
Families have got to stick together.

JENNY
Well, if this is marriage, I want no part of it!

HENRY CLAY
Me either!

SARAH
You'll understand when you're older.

JENNY
Mother, you don't understand! You don't know!

SARAH
Know what?

HENRY CLAY
I saw Mr. Robinson driving....

JENNY
Henry Clay, would you just stay out of this!

SARAH

Now, don't scold him.

JENNY

I can just see this family in Washington! It would be too embarrassing! I would hate it!

SARAH

I wouldn't worry if I were you. In this state, they never elect Republicans to anything—not even dog catcher.

JENNY

Then why is Daddy running for congress if he can't get elected?

SARAH

Ever since your father resigned from government service to come home and help your grandmother in her last days, he's dreamed of one day running for congress, getting into politics, and making a name for himself. This special election gives him a chance.

JENNY

What good is his dream if it never comes true?

SARAH

I guess you have to run with your dreams. That's what dreams are for. We all have to have a dream. All your father's people were high strung, hot tempered, and full of big dreams, just like you and your father.

JENNY

I'm not a thing like Daddy! He doesn't even know who I am! He never listens to a thing I say!

SARAH

Why, your father loves you very much. But it's hard for him to express how he really feels. He's all bottled up—which reminds me of that Elixir.

(Calling loudly.)

Jeff! Jeff!

JEFF

(Entering from the kitchen UR.)

I hear you. I ain't deaf!

SARAH

Jeff, as soon as that Elixir cools you better get it bottled. Hide it on the back porch so it won't disturb Mr. Robinson.

JENNY

Mother! You said you'd get rid of it!

SARAH

Yes, but I didn't say how.

JENNY

Mother!

SARAH

Now, don't worry. What he doesn't know won't hurt him. Here, take this on over to Miz Clifford.

(SARAH hands the bottle to JENNY, who crosses to the hall table, placing the bottle on the table. HENRY CLAY follows her.)

JEFF

If Mr. Robinson finds out you still doin' with that Elixir, look out!

HENRY CLAY
Look out!

SARAH
Why, he's not going to find out, Jeff. It's going to be our little secret.

JEFF
Oh, no, it ain't! I don't want no Mr. Robinson chasing after me about no Elixir! Anyways, time I was getting on down to Memphis. Just stopped off here to rest a spell. How long's it been? Let's see....

SARAH
Let's see—why, you came here in '35. It's been ten years! I can't believe it!

JEFF
Ten years! I weren't planning to stay no ten years.

SARAH
It'll be ten years in September. It was September when you hurt yourself falling off that freight train heading south—and you showed up at my back door needing someplace to rest. Time does go by.

JEFF
It shor do! Ten years! Guess I done rested enough. Time I was gettin' on down to Memphis.

SARAH
Now, Jeff, what would we do without you? Why, you're the best worker I ever had.

JEFF
I weren't planning to be no worker.

SARAH
Why, do you know what you are?

JEFF

No, ma'am.

SARAH

Jeff, you're a—a custodian!

JEFF

Well, I've been cussed enough. But what's an "odian"?

SARAH

A custodian's someone who's—why, in charge!

JEFF

In charge? Of what?

SARAH

Why, all kinds of things! Why, Jeff, you practically run this place.

JEFF

I better run on down to Memphis before Mr. Robinson catches me in charge of that Elixir back there.

SARAH

Now Jeff, you just let me handle Mr. Robinson. From now on you're going to have a new title: Custodian of the Sulphur Spring Inn. Now what do you think of that?

JEFF

Custodian of the Sulphur Spring Inn.... Do a raise go with it?

SARAH

Now, let's not rush into anything. Let's just try out the title for a while—and we can talk about a raise later.

JEFF
Well, talkin' 'bout a raise later is somethin' we done plenty of, that's for dog-gone sure.

SARAH
Well, I'm so glad that's settled.

JEFF
(Mumbling to HIMSELF as he exits UR.)
So I'm in charge, 'cept I ain't in charge of givin' myself no raise. I'm a lucky man!

JENNY
Mother, you are the limit! You can get around anyone—except Daddy. He's your biggest challenge. You're each other's biggest challenge. I still don't understand how you two could ever have gotten married.

SARAH
It was that Miami moon, I guess. Maybe that Miami moon is still casting its spell. So big and yellow. Your father and I walked on the beach under that moon, night after night. Makes people do crazy things.... Your father was like no one I had ever met before. He was in charge of the government office in Miami—used to fly to Cuba in an open cockpit plane, chasing rum runners, tracking down boats sneaking into Miami.

HENRY CLAY
Did he really fly the plane himself?

SARAH
Oh, yes! He wore a helmet and a long white scarf, very dashing. Once he even took me up with him.

JENNY
I can't imagine you doing that!

SARAH

Those were exciting times. Your father—he was so handsome, so dashing, with an eye for the ladies.

JENNY

An eye for the ladies?

HENRY CLAY

I believe that!

SARAH

He could charm the birds out of the trees—when he wanted to. And I was vivacious and full of life in those days. That was a long time ago.

JENNY

You're still vivacious and full of life. You've got more life than anyone I know. Anyone! And the nicest legs! Look, Henry Clay, hasn't she got nice legs?

> (As JENNY lifts the hem of SARAH'S dress, to show a nice pair of legs indeed, JENNY and HENRY CLAY whistle.)

SARAH

> (Playfully slapping JENNY'S hand.)

Stop that!

> (SARAH herself lifts her dress and performs a little dance step.)

They aren't bad, if I do say so myself.

JENNY

I bet you were a flapper. I bet you had lots of boyfriends.

SARAH

I wouldn't be surprised. I had one special boyfriend. He was Greek—a gambler from Coney Island.

HENRY CLAY
Was he really a gambler?

SARAH
Why, no—not really a gambler. I wouldn't call playing poker for money gambling, exactly. He just played a little cards with some of his friends, now and then. But he was always a gentleman and took me to the best places. That was before I met your father. I remember when we used to go dancing at the Steel Pier in Atlantic City.

> (Humming and dancing, SARAH launches into The Charleston. She draws JENNY and HENRY CLAY into the dance and they follow enthusiastically, forming a chorus line. THEY enjoy their dancing for a time, but finally MAY ANNE enters from upstairs.)

MAY ANNE
Will you please tell me what you all are doing?

SARAH
> (As THEY continue to dance.)

Just acting like fools.

MAY ANNE
Where is Tom?

JENNY
Doing the hundred yard dash.

MAY ANNE
My heart is breaking and you're dancing and joking!

> (THEY abruptly stop dancing.)

JENNY
It sure makes you feel better.

MAY ANNE
Tom'll never come back. Not to this crazy family.

JENNY
Well, that's another problem solved.

MAY ANNE
Tom is not the problem! I've got to find him!

(MAY ANNE exits DR.)

SARAH
(Calling after HER.)
Bring Tom back here when you find him.
(To JENNY.)
She always takes things so hard.

(The phone RINGS.)

JENNY
I'll get it.... Sulphur Spring Inn.... Oh, hello, Miz Banks. Just a minute.
(Holding HER hand over the mouthpiece and speaking to SARAH.)
It's Henry Clay's aunt—old Miz Moneybags.

SARAH
Shhhh! She'll hear you!

JENNY
She wants to speak to her sister.

SARAH
Tell her—wait. Let me talk to her.
(SARAH takes the phone from JENNY and speaks into it.)

Hello, how are you, Miz Money Banks? I mean—Miz Banks.... Yes. Do you want to talk to her?
>(To HENRY CLAY.)

Henry Clay, run upstairs and tell your mother her sister is on the phone.
>(HENRY CLAY exits up the stairs. SARAH is again speaking into the phone.)

Henry Clay is calling her.... Well, she has been about the same. She just stays in her room. She won't even come down to eat. I send food up, but she just pecks at it.... Drinking? Well, I wouldn't call it drinking, exactly. She does take a drop now and again. It's for—her arthritis, she says.... Oh, I see. Well, maybe that would be for the best.... You want me to tell her...? We'll have her all packed and ready.... Goodbye.
>(SARAH hangs up the phone.)

Miz Banks is coming Wednesday to take Miz Wood and Henry Clay home with her.

JENNY
Oh, no! Henry Clay will hate that! He says his aunt is so bossy and watches him like a hawk! He'll just hate it!

SARAH
I know. That boy is so high strung. We won't mention it, just yet. Remember, not a word.

JENNY
Okay. But Henry Clay will hate it! And I hate it! I don't want him to go.

HENRY CLAY
>(Entering down the stairs.)

She doesn't feel like coming down.

SARAH
That's all right. Your aunt said—she'd be back in touch.
>(Calling.)

Jeff! Jeff! Where is that Jeff?

(SARAH exits into the kitchen UR.)

JENNY
I—I like you, Henry Clay.

HENRY CLAY
I like you.

JENNY
I'll really miss you, when you go away.

HENRY CLAY
I'm not going away.

JENNY
Everybody goes away—sometime.

HENRY CLAY
Not me. I like it here.

JENNY
I know.

JEFF
(Entering at the "front door" DR.)
Henry Clay, this is the first time I ever seen you standin' still!

JENNY
Jeff, Momma wants you to take this Elixir over to Miz Clifford.

JEFF
Oh, no, she don't. She ask you to take it.

JENNY
Well, it was just a try. Nothing ventured, nothing gained.

JEFF

You shor lost on that one.

JENNY

Here, Jeff, have a piece of candy. It's your raise.

(SHE hands candy to both HENRY CLAY and JEFF.)

JEFF
(Taking the candy.)

Somethin' beats nothin'. You better not let you Momma catch you eatin' this here candy before supper.

JENNY

I'll tell her you gave it to me.

JEFF

That would be a lie.

JENNY

A lie is when you do it for spite. When you can't help it, it isn't a lie.

JEFF

Well, you ought to know.

SARAH
(Calling from the kitchen UR.)

Jeff! Jeff!

JEFF

The way that woman hollers, you'd think I was in Memphis.

SARAH
(Entering from the kitchen UR.)

Jeff, you better come in here and help Aunt Martha, and then I want you to run on to the drug store before supper.

JEFF
(As HE exits through the dining room UC into the kitchen.)
Sure glad I'm in charge!

SARAH
Jenny, you better take that Elixir on over to Miz Clifford.

HENRY CLAY
I'll go with you!

SARAH
No, Henry Clay. I want you to go upstairs and try to get your mother to come down to supper. We'd better get some food into her before—well, never mind. Go on now.
(Reluctantly, HENRY CLAY exits up the stairs.)
Now, go on, Jenny.

(SARAH hands JENNY the Elixir.)

JENNY
Oh, Mother! I was going to shave my legs.

SARAH
You're too young to shave your legs.

JENNY
Just look at them! They're all hairy!

SARAH
They've been hairy for fourteen years. They can be hairy another few minutes. Now go on.

JENNY
Momma, would you have Jeff get me a box of Kotex when he goes to the drug store?

SARAH

You came right by the drug store coming home from school. Why didn't you get it yourself?

JENNY

You have to ask Mr. Wetmore for everything. "Mr. Wetmore, could I have a box of Kotex?" It's too embarrassing.

SARAH

There's nothing to be embarrassed about.

JENNY

Then why did you cry when I started having my period?

SARAH

I hated to think of you grown up enough to need Kotex.

JENNY

I have to grow up sometime, but I'm not ready to ask Mr. Wetmore for Kotex.

SARAH

Oh, all right. Go on now. Don't let Miz Clifford feed you any cake before supper and spoil your appetite.

JENNY

Oh, I won't.

(JENNY puts a piece of candy in her mouth, then exits through the "front door" DR, carrying the Elixir. JEFF enters the dining room UC from the kitchen, carrying dishes which he puts on the table.)

SARAH

Jeff, when you go over to the drug store, get some Kotex.

                          JEFF
Kotex?!

                          SARAH
You know. A box of twelve.

                          JEFF
Looks like women could buy they own Kotex. Men don't need Kotex. Why do men have to buy it?

              (HE exits into the kitchen UR.)

                          SARAH
              (Exiting UC and following JEFF into the kitchen.)
It's the war, I guess.

                          KEENE
              (Entering at the "front door" DR.)
Hello...anyone?

              (Seeing no one, HE turns on the radio.)

                    VOICE ON RADIO
The remnants of the German Army are scattered over Europe. Sporadic fighting continues, particularly in and around Berlin. Patton's Third Army has resumed its offensive into Austria, while British forces have occupied Hamburg, Germany's second largest city.

              (KEENE turns off the radio. HENRY CLAY enters
              from upstairs and tries to sneak out the "front door"
              without KEENE seeing him.)

                          KEENE
              (Seeing HENRY CLAY.)
Henry Clay, how are you?

HENRY CLAY
(Not enthusiastic about being waylaid.)
I'm all right, I guess.

SARAH
(Entering through the dining room UC.)
Sgt. Keene. You're early.

KEENE
How are you today, Madame Sarah?

SARAH
It's been one of those days.
(HENRY CLAY is again edging toward the door.)
Henry Clay, is your mother coming down for supper?

HENRY CLAY
Maybe.

(HE starts to exit DR, but SARAH stops him.)

SARAH
Did she really say, "Maybe"?

HENRY CLAY
I'm not sure. It was either maybe or no.

SARAH
Henry Clay, you are the limit. Now you wait just a minute. I—I want to go up with you to talk to your mother.

HENRY CLAY
Oh, rats!

(HENRY CLAY sits.)

SARAH
How are things out at the hospital?

KEENE
The usual snafu.

SARAH
Are you planning on being here for supper?

KEENE
Yes, if it's convenient for you and Aunt Martha.

SARAH
You know she always puts your name in the pot. She's baked your favorite apple pie.

KEENE
Madame Sarah, it's been kind of you to have me here. You've always made me feel at home. You have a warm heart in a cold world. I value that.

SARAH
We all enjoy having you, and Jenny thinks you hung the moon.
                    (A slow take.)
It's been kind of us to have you? Are you—telling me something?

KEENE
I got my orders today. I'm being transferred.

SARAH
Transferred? Oh, no.

HENRY CLAY
Does that mean you're leaving?

KEENE
I'm afraid so.

HENRY CLAY
(Happy about the news and not able to hide it.)
Oh, that's too bad. Guess you won't be around here anymore.

SARAH
Where will they send you?

KEENE
Probably Germany. They'll need translators during the Occupation.

SARAH
When do you have to go?

KEENE
The middle of next week.

SARAH
We'll all be so sorry to see you go. Jenny will be very upset. She'll miss you very much.

KEENE
And I shall miss her very much—and you. You have been kind to me, Sarah.

SARAH
There's so much trouble and suffering in the world—so many people here a while, then there a while—no home to go home to.... We need to be kind to each other.... Don't tell Jenny yet that you'll be leaving. Let her enjoy tonight—your being here for supper and all.

HENRY CLAY
I can tell her. I don't mind.

SARAH
Henry Clay, don't say a word to Jenny about this. Let her enjoy tonight. Now promise!

HENRY CLAY
(As HE crosses toward DR.)
Oh, all right. I promise. Can I go now? I want to find Jenny.

SARAH
Well, go on. We'll talk to your mother later. Now remember your promise.
(HENRY CLAY exits by the "front door" DR.)
Henry Clay is leaving, too. His aunt is coming to take Henry Clay and his mother home with her, but he doesn't know that yet. I'll tell them later, after supper.

KEENE
It seems to be a time for saying goodbye.

SARAH
Yes, it is. Sergeant, I have a favor to ask.

KEENE
Name it.

SARAH
May Anne's Tom just showed up with a three-day pass. He won't go back out to the hospital tonight because he's afraid that Sgt. Myers will think up something to keep him there. I don't know where I'm going to put him overnight.... He's being sent overseas, too, and he's asked May Anne to marry him before he goes. If I can just get the two of them calmed down. They're both so young to be getting married.

KEENE
What can I do to help?

SARAH
Would you mind if we put a roll-away bed in your room so Tom could have a place to stay?

KEENE
Anything you say, Sarah, but I don't think sharing a room with me is exactly what Tom has in mind.

SARAH
I know what he has in mind, and that's why I thought you could keep an eye on him.

KEENE
For you, Madame Sarah, I'll try anything, including chaperoning a twenty-year-old Corporal who wants to get married before he goes overseas.

SARAH
Thank you, Sergeant. I knew I could count on you.
        (MAY ANNE and TOM enter from the kitchen UR.)
Why, where have you two been?

MAY ANNE
We were just sitting out there by the spring, talking.

SARAH
You should have given Tom some of that sulphur water. That would have cooled him off.

MAY ANNE
Mother!

SARAH
I mean, slowed you down. Well, you know what I mean.

TOM
Yes, ma'am.

SARAH
Anyway, Sgt. Keene here is going to help us.

MAY ANNE
Oh, Sergeant! Can you really help us?

TOM
You don't know how much I'd appreciate it, Sergeant.

KEENE
Oh, I think I do know.

SARAH
We have it all worked out. We're going to put that roll-away bed in Sgt. Keene's room.

TOM
(Disgustedly.)
In Sgt. Keene's room!

SARAH
Sgt. Keene was nice enough to offer to share his room with you, so you wouldn't want him to think you didn't appreciate it, now would you?

KEENE
You wouldn't want that, now would you, Corporal?

TOM
No, Sergeant.

SARAH
(To MAY ANNE.)
What did you do with that roll-away bed?

MAY ANNE
I pushed it all the way out to the gazebo.

SARAH
Well, you better go on and get that bed. And remember, supper

will be ready in a little while—so don't do anything in that gazebo I wouldn't do.

MAY ANNE

Mother!

SARAH

That roll-away bed should keep you busy. I mean—just move it. Don't use it.

MAY ANNE

Mother!

SARAH

Well, you know what I mean.

TOM

Yes, ma'am.

(SARAH exits into the kitchen UR. MAY ANNE and TOM exit by the French doors UL. JENNY and HENRY CLAY enter by the "front door" DR.)

JENNY

Oh, Sgt. Keene!

KEENE

Comment allez-vous, mademoiselle?

JENNY

Très bien, Monsieur. Comment allez-vous?

KEENE

Bien, merci.

HENRY CLAY
(Throwing HIMSELF onto the sofa in disgust.)
Comment allez-vous! Whoopdy, doopdy, do!

JENNY
(Ignoring HENRY CLAY.)
Will you be here for supper?

KEENE
Yes, I am looking forward to having supper with you.

JENNY
I'm so glad to see you! I'm so glad you're staying for supper!

HENRY CLAY
(Overcome with jealousy.)
Oh, rats! Rats! Rats!

(HE runs out the "front door" DR. SARAH enters from the kitchen, bringing flowers to the dining table UC. During the dialogue which follows, SHE remains in the dining room, arranging the flowers.)

SARAH
Sergeant, when you're here is the only time Jenny will sit at the table and actually eat for a change.... Don't you think she's too thin?

JENNY
Mother!

KEENE
No, she's just fine. She looks like a hamadryad or an ondine—just what a young poet should look like.

SARAH
My, that is poetic.

(SHE exits into the kitchen UR.)

JENNY
What's a hamadryad or an ondine?

KEENE
A hamadryad is a wood nymph, and an ondine, a nymph of the sea. You always look on the point of flight—into the shadows of a wood or into the air.

JENNY
Are there other nymphs?

KEENE
Yes, and they are all elemental spirits of earth, air, fire, and water. Which would you choose to be? Earth, air, fire, or water?

JENNY
Air! I would fly away and not be tied down. I would be a nymph of the air and ride on the March wind.

KEENE
Yes, I think that suits you.

JENNY
If I'm an elemental spirit, what is Momma?

KEENE
(Accenting the last syllable: mu-mä´.)
Your Mama is hearth and home and daily bread. She is Demeter, Mother of Earth and Grain, and you are her daughter, Persephone, just stepping onto the fields of spring.

JENNY
The fields of spring....

KEENE
Come, fill the Cup, and in the Fire of Spring
The Winter Garment of Repentance fling!
The Bird of Time has but a little way
To fly—and Lo! the Bird is on the Wing.

JENNY
That is so beautiful. Who wrote it?

KEENE
It's from *The Rubáiyát of Omar Khayyám*. He was a poet in ancient Persia.

JENNY
(In wonder.)
In ancient Persia....

KEENE
He lived 900 years ago.

JENNY
Those were his feelings 900 years ago, and they are still alive. And now you are saying them to me.

KEENE
Yes.

JENNY
I—wrote a poem and—dedicated it to you. Would you like to hear it?

KEENE
Yes, I would.

(JENNY pulls a paper out of her bobby sock.)

                    JENNY
I stood on the highest hill.
The wind blew back my hair.
I watched the sun go down.
I watched the colors flare.

I knew the next sun that rose
Would look on a different place.
I knew the sun would see on this hill
A new and different face.

I looked at the flowers
In a basket at my feet.
I picked a violet from the bunch,
And it smelled sweet.

I did not look for the moon.
I did not want it yet.
I picked up my basket of flowers
And walked into the sunset.

Do you like it?

                    KEENE
Very much.

                    JENNY
I could give you a copy—if you want me to.

                    KEENE
Yes, I'd like that.
            (JENNY takes a second copy of the poem out of
            one of her bobby socks and gives it to KEENE.)
When I read it, I will think of my young friend who made me re‐
member my own youth.

JENNY

What was it like—growing up in Paris?

KEENE

In the '20s, all of Paris seemed young, perhaps because I was young. All of Paris seemed in bloom, flowers everywhere and the air like wine. But the Paris I knew is gone. It seems a very long time ago.

JENNY

But you're not old.

KEENE

I'm thirty-nine. Almost forty.

JENNY

Forty! But you don't look that old. I mean—you don't seem that old. You're only—twenty-five years older than I am. That's not that much difference.

KEENE

It seems a very long time since I was your age. It was in another county and another time.

JENNY

Oh, don't say that. It makes me feel sad. As if—as if it had already been lived—and is gone.

KEENE

Everything is lived, and gone—too soon.

JENNY

I've wanted to ask someone, but there was no one to ask.... You always listen to me. You really listen. Will you not laugh at me?

KEENE

I would never laugh at you.

JENNY

Well, then—do you think an older man could be attracted to someone younger? I'm asking for a friend.

KEENE

A friend about your age?

JENNY

Yes, about my age.

KEENE

And the older man?

JENNY

Well, he doesn't look forty—not as old as you are.

KEENE

That's a comfort to know. Would someone older, though he doesn't look forty, be attracted to someone like you, for instance?

JENNY

Oh, I'm not talking about me.

KEENE

It's—your friend.

JENNY

Yes, a friend of mine. I was just wondering—she was just wondering. Well, she won't always be fourteen.

KEENE

No, she won't always be fourteen. I think anyone would be attracted to a friend like you. To life—to the fountain of youth.

JENNY
But I mean—more than that. Do people who are years older ever—marry people who are years younger?

KEENE
Sometimes friendship lasts longer—remembering when you are years older the kindness of your young friend.

JENNY
But then there's nothing to hope for, or hold on to.

KEENE
Jenny, you have to be willing to let go. To enjoy, and then to let them go. To wish them well—and au revoir. Do you understand?

JENNY
I guess so. I'm not sure.... Thank you for listening.... I can always talk to you. I'm sorry that you're almost forty.

KEENE
So am I.
    (HENRY CLAY peeks in the French doors UL, making it clear that he has been eavesdropping.)
I'm going upstairs to freshen up. Would you like to play checkers after supper?

JENNY
Oh, yes, I'd like that. I'll get them ready.

KEENE
You're on.

    (HE exits up the stairs. JENNY gets out the checkers and the board from the desk drawer and puts them on the coffee table.)

SARAH
(Entering the dining room UC from the kitchen.)
Jenny, will you help set the table?

JENNY
Oh, Mother, I was going to set up the checkers. Sgt. Keene and I are going to play after supper.

SARAH
It won't take a minute to set the table.

(SARAH and JENNY exit through the dining room UC, as HENRY CLAY enters UL. HE crosses immediately to the checkerboard.)

HENRY CLAY
Comment allez-vous—to you!

(HENRY CLAY picks up the checkers and throws them into the fireplace then hurriedly crosses to DR, just as JEFF enters DR carrying twelve boxes of Kotex and other packages. The distinctive, readily-recognizable blue Kotex boxes of the period are duplicated. As JEFF enters and is bumped by HENRY CLAY, the stack of boxes tilts. JEFF tries to keep them from falling, but they do, scattering across the expanse of the floor.)

JEFF
Whoa there, Hoss.

(HENRY CLAY hurriedly exits DR.)

SARAH
(Entering the dining room UC from the kitchen.)
Jeff, what is all that?

JEFF

Looks like twelve boxes of Kotex all over the floor.

SARAH

Twelve boxes! Why in the world did you buy twelve boxes of Kotex?

JEFF

You told me to get twelve.

SARAH

Oh, my, I said a box of twelve, not twelve boxes. Good heavens, they'll think we've got a flood over here.

JEFF

They shor will.

SARAH

Let's get these boxes back there in the pantry before Jenny sees them. I can just hear her now, "Oh, Mother, how could you?" She already thinks I belong out at Darnell Hospital.... Twelve boxes! Oh, my! They'll think we've got a flood, for sure!

(SARAH is picking up the boxes and stacking them back into JEFF'S arms, as JENNY enters through the dining room UC.)

JENNY

Mother! What is all of that!

SARAH

It looks like twelve boxes of Kotex all over the floor.

JENNY

Oh, Mother! How could you? Sgt. Keene is coming back down in a minute.

SARAH
You wanted Jeff to buy you some Kotex. Well, here it is.

(SARAH hands JENNY one of the boxes.)

JENNY
Do you have to announce it to the entire world? "Look, everybody, twelve boxes of Kotex on the living room floor!"
    (SHE holds the box high.)
"And one of them is mine!" Sometimes I think everybody in this house is crazy but me!

    (Carrying the box, SHE heads for the stairs. MAY ANNE and TOM enter the "front door" DR, MAY ANNE pulling and TOM pushing the bed.)

MAY ANNE
(As SHE passes JENNY.)
What's the matter with you?
    (JENNY exits upstairs without answering. MAY ANNE addresses TOM.)
She's always in a huff about something.... Mother, where do you want this?
    (Noticing the Kotex.)
Mother, what are you doing with that, all over the floor?

SARAH
Well, I'm picking it up.

TOM
Can I help you, Miz Robinson?
    (TOM picks up one of the boxes and starts to add it to JEFF'S stack.)

MAY ANNE

Tom! Put that down!

 (TOM drops the box to the floor as he would a hot potato.)

This family is so embarrassing!

 (Abandoning the bed DR, MAY ANNE exits through the French doors UL.)

TOM

 (As HE hurries after her, also exiting UL.)

May Anne! May Anne!

 (SARAH has resumed the task of picking the boxes up from the floor and stacking them into JEFF'S arms.)

JEFF

Like you keep saying....

SARAH and JEFF

It's the war, I guess.

BLACKOUT

END of ACT I

Period MUSIC is played during intermission.

ACT II: SCENE ONE

(It is the same afternoon, a few minutes later. SARAH and JEFF are gone, as is the Kotex. The rollaway bed is where it was last seen DR. JENNY enters from upstairs. She crosses to the checker board and looks around, trying to find the checkers.)

JENNY
Where are those checkers? They were right here.
    (Having looked all around, discovering the checkers in the fireplace.)
Who would throw those checkers in the fireplace? Henry Clay!
    (SHE moves toward the French doors UL.)
Henry Clay! Did you throw those checkers in the fireplace? Henry Clay!

    (SHE exits by the French doors UL, as MAY ANNE and TOM enter through the French doors UL.)

MAY ANNE
We'd better get Jeff to help us get that bed upstairs.

TOM
We can do it! You'll see!
    (MAY ANNE and TOM cross to the bed, where they stand on opposite sides of the bed, gazing into one another's eyes. HE suddenly draws HER away from the bed. Both cross to DC.)
May Anne, I love you! I need you! I want you!

MAY ANNE
Oh, Tom. I love you! I need you! I want you!
    (THEY kiss.)
But I don't know if I can marry you right now.

TOM

Oh, May Anne, if you don't marry me, right now, I may go overseas and get killed! We'd never see each other again!

MAY ANNE

Oh, Tom! Killed?

TOM

Yes! Killed! All of me—dead!
    (HIS glance centers on his crotch.)
I want to make love to you before I go. Oh, May Anne, please marry me!

MAY ANNE

How can I marry you when my father won't even let me go out with you?

TOM

You can't marry me?

MAY ANNE

No.

TOM
(Without much hope.)
Well—would you just sleep with me?

MAY ANNE

Tom! Without being married?

TOM

It was just a thought.

MAY ANNE

If I slept with you before we were married, I wouldn't be a virgin. You wouldn't want to marry someone who wasn't a virgin, would you?

TOM
Oh, no! How could you think that of me!

MAY ANNE
You're a virgin, aren't you?

TOM
A virgin? What does that mean, exactly?

MAY ANNE
You know what a virgin is. Someone who's never been with someone—like that. You know.

TOM
Oh, that kind of virgin.

MAY ANNE
You've never been with anyone—like that—have you?

TOM
Oh, no! Does my sister's best friend count?

MAY ANNE
Your sister's best friend! Tom! You didn't!

TOM
No, I didn't.... She did.

MAY ANNE
Tom! ... What was it—like?

TOM
It was—terrific!

MAY ANNE
Terrific?!

TOM

Terrifically—awful!
            (HE gesticulates rejection.)
Awful! . . . Awful!

MAY ANNE

Awful?

TOM

I mean—awfully—interesting.

MAY ANNE

Interesting? Just—interesting?

TOM

Kind of—stimulating. Intellectually stimulating.

MAY ANNE

Intellectually stimulating?

TOM

Well, not just—intellectually stimulating.... All kinds of stimulating!
            (For a long moment, TOM stares lustfully at MAY ANNE, ready to pounce. MAY ANNE'S reaction is avidly anticipatory.)
Oh, May Anne!
            (HE springs at HER and holds her tight.)
Let's go upstairs and I'll show you!

            (THEY kiss with increased passion.)

JENNY
            (Entering from DR.)
That looks like fun.

(MAY ANNE and TOM, a bit rumpled, break apart.)

MAY ANNE
We're having a serious discussion.

JENNY
I can see that. I didn't have that much fun when I was kissed.

MAY ANNE
When were you ever kissed?

JENNY
You don't know everything about me. Roy Lee James grabbed me on the way home from school and kissed me. But it wasn't as much fun as what you are doing.

MAY ANNE
What we are doing is none of your business.

JENNY
Even I could figure that out.

MAY ANNE
Would you mind just going back outside?

JENNY
Oh, I don't mind. I'm looking for Henry Clay.

MAY ANNE
We'll let you know when we're finished.

JENNY
Well, I can't stay outside all night.

(SHE exits DR.)

TOM

May Anne, what am I going to do? If you don't marry me, I'll—shoot myself!

MAY ANNE

Shoot yourself?

TOM

In the foot!

(HE enacts the shot—foot held high.)

MAY ANNE

Oh, Tom! You wouldn't!

TOM

No, I wouldn't. But I'd feel like it. Life without you would be like shooting myself in the foot.

MAY ANNE

But, Tom, I don't know what it's like to be married. One day you're not married, and then the next day, you are.... I wouldn't know how to act.

TOM

I guess you just learn as you go along.

MAY ANNE

But Tom, if you go overseas, and then you're killed, why, we couldn't learn anything. I'd just be a widow! I'm too young to be a widow!

TOM

I promise you I won't get killed! If you're waiting for me, I know I'll come back!

MAY ANNE

Will you? Promise?

TOM

Oh, May Anne! I'll promise anything.

    (THEY kiss again.)

Let's get this bed upstairs, so we can—talk about it some more.

    (THEY cross to the bed and, experiencing great difficulty, manage to get one end of the bed up only a step or two—MAY ANNE on the stairs lifting, and TOM pushing from below.)

MAY ANNE

Push when I lift!

TOM

Lift when I push!

MAY ANNE

Now—push!

TOM

Now—lift!

JENNY

    (Entering DR and hurriedly pushing the bed back into the hallway.)

Quick! Push it into the kitchen!

MAY ANNE

No! We're taking it upstairs!

JENNY

There isn't time! Daddy just got out of his car, and he's coming up the walk!

MAY ANNE
Oh, no! Tom! Push it into the kitchen! Jenny, you stay here and head him off.

(MAY ANNE and TOM, pushing the bed, exit into the kitchen UR.)

JENNY
Why am I always in the middle of everything? Why?

(EVAN enters by the "front door" DR, out of breath. He manages to cross to a chair and sit. JENNY hurries to his side.)

Daddy! Are you all right? You look so pale!

EVAN
I'm all right—just winded.

JENNY
I'd better call Momma.

EVAN
No, don't call her. I need one of these pills, that's all.

(HE puts a pill into his palm.)

Just get me a glass of water.

(Trying to respond as quickly as possible, JENNY grabs the glass of sulphur water from the radio, and hands it to EVAN. He takes the pill, then drinks the water. Realizing in disgust it's the sulphur water, he spits part of it out.)

That damned sulphur water!

JENNY
Momma says it's good for you.

EVAN
It stinks and it tastes terrible.

JENNY
I know.

EVAN
Leaving that water around where innocent people can drink it! That woman will be the—death of me yet!

JENNY
Daddy—you're... you're not—really ill, are you?

EVAN
Now, don't look so worried. I'm all right.
>   (HE puts his head back against the chair.)

Just need to rest a little.

JENNY
>   (Very concerned.)

I better call Momma.

EVAN
No, I'm all right. Just stay here by me, Jenny.
>   (HE takes JENNY'S hand as she sits on the footstool by his chair. He rests for a long moment, then he looks at her.)

Just once in a while—I've been feeling a little light-headed.

JENNY
Are you feeling better now?

EVAN
Yes. That doctor doesn't know everything....

JENNY
What did the doctor say?

EVAN

Take it easy. Slow down. How can I take it easy when I'm running for congress?

JENNY

Maybe you ought to take it easy like the doctor says.

EVAN

What do they expect me to do? Crawl into my grave? When I go, it's with my boots on.

JENNY

Running for your dream.

EVAN

That's right, Jenny. Running for my dream! You've got a good head on your shoulders.
    (HE settles back, resting.)
Now, not a word of this to your mother.... I don't want any of her fussing around.

JENNY

But, Daddy....

EVAN

I'm all right. Your mother has enough on her mind. She works from morning to night as it is. She doesn't need this to worry about.... Now, don't say anything to her. Give me your word.

JENNY

I won't say anything.

EVAN

Do you remember, Jenny, when I used to take you and Andrew hunting? There seemed to be so much time then.

JENNY

I remember.

EVAN

And sometimes it would just be you and me.... You were only seven or eight.... The men would sit around the campfire, swapping stories and listening to the voices of the hounds—the bell tone of Lady—remember? She only had three legs. One got tore off in a fence.... But she had twelve puppies at one time—prettiest puppies I ever did see.... The deep sound of Big Blue, far away beyond the hills. They're all dead and gone.... We're the only ones who remember their names.

JENNY

I remember.

EVAN

I remember the day you were born, right here in this house. I was sitting down here, in this chair, and I heard a baby cry and I rushed upstairs. The nurse brought you out and I said some fool thing like, "Whose baby is that?" Then she held you out to me, "Why, this is your little girl," she said, and I held you in my arms—such tiny fingers and toes, but they were all there. Such a feeling of—joy!
        (HIS hand touches JENNY'S head lovingly.)
I want you to go off to college, get out of this town, see something of the world—and be somebody I can be proud of.

JENNY

Yes, sir, I will.

EVAN

I know you will. You look after things around here, Jenny, 'til Andrew comes home. Your mother has got a good heart. They broke the mold when they made her.... But your mother's got a screw loose somewhere.

JENNY
Yes, sir.

EVAN
Now go out to the car and get those things I brought over—some ration coupons, eggs, and whatever else Ezra put in that sack on the back seat.

JENNY
Daddy—are you really all right?

EVAN
I'm really all right. Now go on.

(JENNY exits by the "front door" DR. EVAN rises and stands DC, looking over the heads of the audience as if he is looking out a window.)

SARAH
(Entering through the French doors UL, carrying freshly-picked flowers.)
Why, Evan! Is anything the matter?

EVAN
I'm looking out the window. Why does that make something the matter?

SARAH
You seem so—quiet.

EVAN
I was just—remembering. I had a tree house over there, in that horse chestnut tree.

SARAH
I remember your mother telling me about that tree house—how

you had built it from bits and pieces of wood you found all over town—and how all the other boys envied the good job you'd done. Your mother was so proud of you!

EVAN
Yes, God bless her.... You were kind to my mother, Sarah, those last years when she needed you.

SARAH
I remember how kind she was to me when you and I were first married. I was just a stranger—from a different religion, different people—but she took me in.

EVAN
She wanted us to be happy.... I used to wonder—did she ever really understand how a Jewish girl from Coney Island and a Scotch-Irishman from Kentucky came under the spell of that Miami moon? How that moon made everything seem—so simple.

SARAH
That Miami moon—so big and full—casting its spell.

EVAN
We used to walk on the beach under that moon, night after night.

SARAH
Just happy to be together.

EVAN
Yes, happy to be together.... A lot of water's gone under the bridge since then.

SARAH
Yes. It was a long time ago.

EVAN

Sarah, I haven't done what I thought I would with my life.... I had such dreams of what I would do. And it all seemed so simple. So simple.
   (After a thoughtful pause.)
And after I had done all those things I was going to do, I was going to write my memoirs—so it wouldn't all be forgotten.... And now it's almost over—and in my memoirs—blank pages! ... Blank pages!

SARAH

You left your government career to come home to care for your mother. We cared for her together. And we've been a family with three fine children. Those pages are not blank. They are filled with love and caring.

EVAN

I wish I had been more loving and caring. And less....
   (Pause.)
Damn fool notion running for congress!

SARAH

You're got to run with your dreams.

EVAN

Jenny just said that.

SARAH

And there's always time—for your dreams.

EVAN

Yes, still time.... Sarah, I want you to know—Lucille—had to be. I—can't put it into words, but it—had to be.
   (Pause.)
But Lucille isn't....

SARAH

I know, Evan.

EVAN

I haven't been the best husband for you. Too cranky. Too—unsettled.... You should have left me, and left this town, a long time ago. Made a different life for yourself. Gone back to your own people. Why didn't you?

SARAH

Families have got to stick together.... When I think of the war over there in Europe, I think of the families over there, wandering the roads, with no place to go home to and no one to care. Not even knowing if their loved ones are alive or dead.... Families have got to stick together. All we've got is each other.

EVAN

Sometimes we learn that too late.

SARAH

Evan, it's never too late.... There's something I want you to know....

EVAN
 (HE speaks tenderly, but is experiences difficulty in expressing what he feels.)
Sarah, there's something more I want you to know....

 (EVAN is trying to find the words as JENNY, carrying a sack, enters at the "front door" DR, inadvertently breaking the spell.)

JENNY
 (Holding up the sack.)
Where do you want this?

EVAN

Here, I'll take it.
    (EVAN takes the sack from JENNY.)
There are some extra ration coupons in here, and some eggs, just laid this morning. I don't know what else. Ezra packed it.

SARAH

Why, wasn't that nice of him.

EVAN

I'll just take it back to the kitchen.

JENNY

Oh, no, Daddy! I can take it!

    (JENNY tries to take the sack from EVAN, but he refuses to relinquish it.)

EVAN

I'm not an invalid yet!

    (Carrying the sack, EVAN exits through the dining room UC, into the kitchen UR.)

JENNY

    (Loudly, intending to be heard in the kitchen.)
Daddy, you don't have to carry that into the kitchen!
    (In a stage whisper.)
Momma! The roll-away bed!

    (JENNY quickly follows EVAN, exiting UC.)

SARAH

Oh, good Lord!
    (MAY ANNE and TOM enter the hall UR, frantically pushing the roll-away bed. Crossing, SARAH

hurriedly covers TOM'S head with the bed cover.)
Go out the front door!

> (TOM in front, hidden from the rear by both the bed and the bedcover, and MAY ANNE behind, pushing, manage to get the bed through the "front door" DR, just as EVAN enters from the kitchen UR. TOM has exited. All EVAN sees is the bed at the DR wing and MAY ANNE, her back to the bed, facing Evan.)

EVAN
Sarah! What is going on here?

SARAH
Why, it's just a roll-away bed.

EVAN
May Anne! In the name of God, where are you going with that bed?

MAY ANNE
(Wide-eyed and vaguely.)
Where am I going? I don't know.

> (MAY ANNE, walking backwards, exits DR with the bed.)

EVAN
Sarah, where is she going with that bed?

SARAH
With that bed? Why, it just needs a little airing. I just told her to push it around in the yard a little bit.

EVAN

Sarah, sometimes I think you are going nuts.

SARAH

Sometimes I think I am, too.

(JENNY enters UR.)

EVAN

Jenny, what do you know about that roll-away bed?

JENNY

What roll-away bed?

EVAN

The one arrested for speeding.

JENNY

I haven't seen a thing.

EVAN

I don't know why May Anne has to push that bed around in the yard! But if she's got to do it, go out there and help get it over with—before the whole town realizes this family's nuttier than anyone out at Darnell!

JENNY

Yes, sir.

(JENNY exits DR.)

EVAN

For a moment, Sarah—only a moment—I was beginning to remember what attracted me to you a long time ago. But, thank God, you always do one more damn fool thing that brings me back to my senses.

SARAH
Now, Evan, don't get all excited.

EVAN
(Intensely agitated.)
I am not excited!

SARAH
Let me fix you a nice hot cup of sassafras tea.

EVAN
I do not want a nice hot cup of sassafras tea.

SARAH
It'll calm your nerves.

EVAN
I do not want my nerves calm! If I wanted my nerves calm, I'd stay a mile away from this place! Goodbye!

(EVAN exits, storming out the "front door" DR.)

JEFF
(Entering from the dining room UC.)
Aunt Martha's hotter'n that stove back there 'cause you people keeps runnin' that bed through her kitchen like it's the Kentucky Derby.

SARAH
It's all right, Jeff. I'll go help Aunt Martha. Remember to put that Elixir on the back porch to cool, but first get that bed back into the house. Bring it in the front door.... No use upsetting Aunt Martha any more than we have already.

JEFF
I can't figure what they doin' with that bed out in the yard. They ain't no sense to it—none!

SARAH

It's the war, Jeff. It's the war.

(SARAH and JEFF exit through the dining room UC. MAY ANNE and TOM enter through the French doors UL, engaged in a heated discussion.)

TOM

Well, it wasn't my idea to spend my honeymoon in a roll-away bed with Sgt. Keene!

MAY ANNE

Well, just don't try to blame it on me!

JEFF

(Entering UR.)
There you are! Where is that bed?

TOM

Out in the gazebo! Where would you expect a bed to be?

JEFF

I'd 'spect a bed to be in a bedroom. The way I'd 'spect a gah-zee to be in a gazebo!

(HE exits DR.)

MAY ANNE

I think you're afraid to speak to my father.

TOM

Well, let's put it this way. I'd rather face a German Panzer division than speak to your father.... Why don't you speak to your father?

MAY ANNE

You want me to speak to my own father? What a mean thing to say!

TOM
Why do we have to speak to your father? Look, May Anne, we could just go out to the hospital and be married by one of the chaplains—and your father would just find out, afterward—somehow.

MAY ANNE
What do you mean, he'd just find out afterward—somehow?

TOM
We could just get married, and some time when we ran into your father, we could just say, "Hi, Mr. Robinson. How's things? By the way, we got married, a while back, out at the mental hospital."

MAY ANNE
How are we going to happen to run into my father—when you are overseas?

TOM
I mean—whichever one of us happened to run into him.

MAY ANNE
You mean—me!

TOM
Not necessarily, May Anne. Just whichever of us—happened to run into him.... Oh, May Anne! Let's not worry about your father.... I'm not worrying about my father!

MAY ANNE
I don't know your father—but I do know mine. And he's right here!

TOM
But he wouldn't be at the mental hospital—if we got married there!

MAY ANNE
Well—it would be a way to keep him from butting in—being married out there.

TOM
That's what I mean!

MAY ANNE
But where would we go on our honeymoon?

TOM
(After giving it some thought.)
Well—the patients aren't always in their rooms.

MAY ANNE
Tom! Have our honeymoon in some empty room in a mental hospital?
(SHE is aghast—sobbing.)
How could you be so—crude?!

(JEFF enters at the "front door" DR, pushing the roll-away bed.)

JEFF
Where do you want this here bed?

MAY ANNE
I don't want it at all!

(Sobbing, SHE exits up the stairs.)

JEFF
(Turning to TOM.)
Where do you want this here bed?

TOM

I wish someone would take that bed and shove it! May Anne! May Anne!

>(TOM pushes one end of the bed so angrily that it rotates on its casters, as he exits up the stairs. SARAH enters the dining room UC from the kitchen UR. She pauses to rearrange the flowers on the dining room table, then moves downstage, where she sees JEFF leaning on the bed, feigning exhaustion.)

SARAH

Jeff, why are you just standing there leaning on that bed?

JEFF

I can't figure why this bed has been on a merry-go-round all day—and I can't figure why me 'n' this bed's the only ones still on the merry-go-round.

SARAH

Where did Tom get to?

JEFF

When he went upstairs, he told me to take this bed and shove it.

SARAH

Well, you'll need some help for that.
>(Calling upstairs.)
Tom, come on down and help Jeff shove this bed!

TOM

>(From upstairs.)

Yes, ma'am.

>(TOM and KEENE enter from upstairs.)

KEENE

Here, let me help.

(TOM, KEENE, and JEFF exit up the stairs, carrying the bed.)

SARAH

(Crossing to the phone, then speaking into it.)
Hello... Mildred...? Is that you? Did your sister's no-good husband ever come back...? Well, she's better off without him. Would you ring 5868...? Ezra...? There's something I want you to do for me. Mr. Robinson isn't looking as well as he should. Don't let him eat too much of that country ham. It's too salty.... But don't say I said so. You know how he is. Whatever I say he does the opposite.... Thank you, Ezra. Do you still have some of that Elixir...? I'll send you over a few bottles.

(SHE returns the phone to the table. KEENE, TOM, and JEFF enter from upstairs.)

JEFF

Why don't nobody tip nobody around here? In a hotel or an inn— you carry something for somebody, you s'posed to get a tip.... I'll bet down there in Memphis everybody is tipping everybody all the time.

SARAH

Why, you're a custodian now, Jeff. No one tips custodians, not even in Memphis.... Why, custodians are too proud to accept tips!

JEFF

I can see that. It's cause we're in charge.

(SARAH and JEFF exit into the kitchen UR.)

TOM
Sergeant, I'm in desperate trouble. I only have a three-day pass, and I need your advice.

KEENE
What sort of advice?

TOM
Well, I just thought, maybe—you've been around a lot, and you probably know a lot about women....

KEENE
Any man who claims to know a lot about women proves how little he knows.

TOM
Well, May Anne ran upstairs crying. She's locked her door, and she won't speak to me. I'm worse off now than I was when I got here, and I only have a three-day pass! Sergeant, what can I do?

KEENE
Why don't you just go back upstairs, and tell her you're sorry—that it's all your fault?

TOM
But I don't know what I've done.

KEENE
It doesn't matter. By the time you two kiss and make up, she won't remember either.

TOM
Sometimes I think I'll never understand women.

KEENE
You're right. You won't. But it doesn't matter. Go on upstairs. She'll be waiting for you.

TOM
(Solemnly extending HIS hand.)
Thanks, Sergeant!

(THEY shake hands, then TOM excitedly exits up the stairs. JENNY enters through the French doors UL.)

KEENE
Ah, Jenny! Too bad you missed it! I just told Tom everything I know about women. It took less than thirty seconds.

JENNY
Everything I know about men—I've learned from you. And to tell it would take—longer.
(The phone RINGS. SHE answers.)
Sulphur Spring Inn.
(SARAH enters the dining room UC from the kitchen, carrying tableware and condiments which she arranges on the table.)
Yes, he's here. I'll call him.... It's Miss Lee, Sgt. Keene.

(KEENE takes the phone from JENNY, and begins a conversation, facing upstage, his speech not audible to the audience.)

SARAH
(Having moved downstage.)
Well, supper's ready. Where are May Anne and Tom?

JENNY
(Pouting.)
I don't know. They're upstairs, I guess.

SARAH

Good thing supper's ready.... Why, what's the matter?

JENNY

It's that Miss Patricia Lee on the phone. I don't know why she won't leave him alone. She's always calling over here.

SARAH

They're just friends.

JENNY

Mother, don't try to smooth it over. He'd rather be with her than with us, that's all. He'll probably go over there after supper.

SARAH

He thinks the world of you.

JENNY

Well, I don't care! Oh, Mother, just leave me alone.

SARAH

Well, anyhow, supper's ready.
   (Calling.)
May Anne! Tom! Supper's ready!

KEENE
   (Continuing to speak into the phone, but now facing downstage—and now audible.)
Right. See you later. Goodbye.

   (HE returns the phone to the table. MAY ANNE and TOM enter from upstairs.)

MAY ANNE

Mother, Tom and I have definitely decided. We're definitely going to get married.

TOM
(HIS emphatic echoing statement weakening as he observes SARAH'S reaction.)
We're definitely going to... get married.

SARAH
(Not one to be fazed by an ultimatum.)
I know you're going to get married. Why, everybody gets married—some day. We'll talk about it after supper.

(KEENE has quietly crossed to the fireplace DL, where he stands observing.)

MAY ANNE
We're not going to wait until after supper to talk about it! If you won't let us be married here, we're going to go out to the mental hospital and be married by one of the chaplains, and we'll just have to find someplace to stay—out at the mental hospital or—anywhere!

SARAH
Why, you'll do no such thing. Who ever heard of getting married in a mental hospital? You'll be married right here in your own home.

JENNY
The Sulphur Spring Asylum.

MAY ANNE
Oh, Momma! Can we be married here?

SARAH
Why, of course—one of these days.

MAY ANNE
Oh, no you don't. You can get around Daddy like that, but I know you too well. Tom and I want to be married tonight, and at least have our honeymoon before he has to go overseas.

SARAH

Oh, brother.

MAY ANNE

Momma, please help us.

TOM

Please help, Miz Robinson.

SARAH

Tom, you're a very nice young man, and I'm sure you're from a very nice family—but you two have known each other only a few months.

MAY ANNE

You and Daddy only knew each other for three weeks.

SARAH

And you can see how that turned out.

MAY ANNE

Oh, Mother!

SARAH

May Anne, you and Tom are so young.

TOM

We're getting older by the minute, Miz Robinson.

MAY ANNE

Mother, if we don't get married now—and Tom goes overseas and gets killed—I won't even be a widow! And it will all be your fault!

TOM

She won't even be a widow!

MAY ANNE
And it will all be your fault!

SARAH
(After thinking it over.)
Well...that makes sense. But I don't know how we can explain that to your father.

MAY ANNE
Oh, Momma! We'll have to get a minister right away!

JENNY
What minister? Daddy is a fallen-away Baptist, I'm an atheist, you've gone over to tennis lessons, and Momma is her very own Salvation Army.

KEENE
Forgive me. I couldn't help overhearing. I could call the hospital and see if I can get them to send one of the chaplains.

MAY ANNE
Oh, Sergeant! Could you?

KEENE
Let's see what I can do.

(HE crosses to the phone.)

TOM
Thanks, Sergeant!

KEENE
(Into the phone.)
Please ring Darnell Hospital—the Orderly Room.... Gus, Alex Keene here. I have a favor to ask. One of your men—Tom Young—has his orders for shipping out. He's engaged to a young woman

here, and she's crying her eyes out. They want to be married, tonight, and they need a chaplain.... You've got the picture. Can you con one of the chaplains into showing up at the Sulphur Spring Inn about an hour from now...? Thanks, Gus. I'll repay the favor.
   (HE replaces the phone on the table.)
It's all set. Gus said he'd get a chaplain over here if he has to drag him out of the chow line.

MAY ANNE

Oh, Sgt. Keene, you're wonderful! Oh! But where are we going to stay on our honeymoon?

KEENE

Tom already has half of my room. You can have all of it. I'll—make other arrangements.

JENNY

Other arrangements!

MAY ANNE

Oh, Sgt. Keene, you're wonderful! But we don't want to put you out....

KEENE

No problem. I can stay with a friend.

JENNY

Friend!

TOM

Wow! Thanks, Sergeant! If I can ever do anything for you, just tell me!

MAY ANNE

But Momma, how will we tell Daddy?

SARAH

May Anne, do me a favor. Don't mention your father again 'til after supper. For now, what he doesn't know won't hurt him.... Supper's ready, everyone! Jenny, call Henry Clay.

>(MAY ANNE, TOM, KEENE, and SARAH take their places at the dining room table UC. JENNY is crossing toward DR when HENRY CLAY enters DR, running. HE is carrying two large cookies.)

HENRY CLAY

Look what I brought you! Here!

>(HE hands JENNY one of the cookies.)

JENNY

>(Quickly taking a bite of the cookie.)

Henry Clay! You went down to the train station again, didn't you?

HENRY CLAY

I sure did!

JENNY

Those women don't make those cookies for you. They make them for the soldiers on the troop trains!

HENRY CLAY

I'm going to be a soldier! I'm going to be an Air Corps Ace! And they'll pin lots of medals on me! And you'll never see any Sgt. Keene getting any medals pinned on him!

JENNY

I don't want Sgt. Keene getting any medals pinned on him.

HENRY CLAY

You think he's so much! I bet when he—goes away from here, he won't think anything about you.

JENNY

Well, he's not the one who's going away, so there!

HENRY CLAY

That's all you know!

JENNY

That's all you know! You're just a child, Henry Clay. You don't understand any thing about life.

(SHE crosses into the dining room UC.)

HENRY CLAY
(Pausing for momentary introspection.)
Rats! Jenny knows everything—but she needs some instruction!

FADE to DIM.

END of ACT II, SCENE ONE

The FADE to DIM is followed without a time lapse by a FADE IN initiating the action of SCENE TWO.

ACT II: SCENE TWO

(It is an hour later. ALL have finished eating. SARAH, MAY ANNE, TOM, JENNY, HENRY CLAY, and KEENE are moving downstage from the dining room UC as JEFF enters from the kitchen UR, carrying a tray of coffee, cups, and fixings. He puts the tray on the coffee table.)

KEENE
Tell Aunt Martha that was the best apple pie I've ever had.

JEFF
I'll tell her. She made it special for you. Don't nobody make nothin' special for me.

(JEFF exits UR.)

JENNY
Would you like some coffee, Sgt. Keene?

KEENE
Yes, thank you.

(JENNY pours coffee and hands the cup to KEENE.)

JENNY
Momma?

SARAH
Not right now.

JENNY
Here, Henry Clay.

(SHE pours coffee and hands the cup to HENRY CLAY. He makes a show of adding four heaping

spoons of sugar.)
May Anne? Tom?

MAY ANNE
I'll get—ours.
    (Giggling.)
Have to get used to it!

(MAY ANNE pours for TOM and herself.)

KEENE
Jenny and I are going to play checkers, Henry Clay. Would you like to play the winner?

HENRY CLAY
I, ah....

KEENE
(Looking about.)
Where are the checkers?

HENRY CLAY
I, er, ah....

JENNY
The checkers got spilled into the fireplace. By mistake. It was—just an accident.

HENRY CLAY
That's what it was—an accident.

(HE shamefacedly kneels by the fireplace and starts picking up the checkers, blowing ashes off of them as he does.)

MAY ANNE
The chaplain should be here any minute! Sgt. Myers will find a chaplain, won't he?

KEENE
I'm sure he will.

MAY ANNE
Oh, no!

TOM
What's the matter now?

MAY ANNE
I don't have anything to wear. I can't get married in just any old thing.

SARAH
Why didn't I think of that? May Anne, you're right. Tom understands you can't get married in just any old thing. You do understand, don't you, Tom?

TOM
I do?

SARAH
I've got it! I've just thought of something!

MAY ANNE and TOM
You have?

SARAH
You can just postpone it!

MAY ANNE and TOM
Postpone the wedding?

SARAH

Just for a day or two. Just to give us time—to plan everything. The dress, the wedding ceremony, the reception, the honeymoon....

MAY ANNE and TOM

Plan everything?

SARAH

I knew Tom would like the idea.

MAY ANNE

But Momma, if we postpone the wedding, Tom will be gone. I can't have a wedding without a groom.

SARAH

Too bad. It would be so much simpler.

TOM

May Anne, I've just thought of something! You do have a wedding dress!

MAY ANNE

I do?

TOM

I'll always remember the day we met, and the dress you were wearing. I'll never forget that dress as long as I live. It was pink with white ribbons.

MAY ANNE

It was white with pink ribbons.

TOM

I meant—white with pink ribbons. Whenever I think of us getting married, I see you in that dress. May Anne, that will always be—our dress!

MAY ANNE
Oh, Tom! How romantic! Are you really sure?

TOM
I have never been more sure of anything in my life. When I'm far away and all alone, I will always think of you in that dress—pink with white ribbons

MAY ANNE
(Gazing into HIS eyes.)
White with pink ribbons. And you won't ever forget me?

TOM
I'll never forget you in that dress as long as I live.

MAY ANNE
Then I'll go up and put on my wedding dress.

TOM
I'll go with you.

MAY ANNE
No, Tom, you can't go with me. It's unlucky for the groom to see the bride in her wedding dress before the ceremony.

TOM
But I've already seen you in your wedding dress.

MAY ANNE
But it wasn't a wedding dress when you saw it.

(MAY ANNE kisses TOM then exits up the stairs.)

JENNY
Wait! You still have to postpone the wedding, because I don't have anything to wear!

TOM
Jenny, I'll always remember you in—what you're wearing right now.

SARAH
Well, I guess this wedding was meant to be. I always say, just laugh and the world laughs with you; weep and you weep alone.... Tom, why don't you go help Jeff with those bottles? Go on, now. That'll keep you out of mischief.

TOM
Yes, ma'am.

> (TOM exits UR.)

SARAH
Henry Clay, go in and get that tray from Aunt Martha. I had her fix a little something for your mother.
> (After carefully placing the checkers he has been picking up and dusting on the coffee table, HENRY CLAY exits UR. SARAH crosses to the phone, making a call.)

Hello.... Doris...? Is your arthritis any better...? Well, the warm weather'll be here soon.... Will you ring 5868...? Ezra, has Mr. Robinson come home yet...? Well, when he does, would you ask him to stop here on his way to the council meeting? There's just a little something I forgot to tell him.... No, it's a surprise.... I know Mr. Robinson doesn't like surprises—but he's going to get one. Thank you, Ezra. Goodbye.
> (SHE hangs up the phone. HENRY CLAY enters with the tray.)

We'll just take this upstairs.

HENRY CLAY
I was going to play checkers.

SARAH
I know, but there's something I have to tell you and your mother—about your Aunt Eula calling today.

HENRY CLAY
She's going to make us go back and live with her, isn't she?

SARAH
Yes, I'm afraid so.

HENRY CLAY
I don't want to go.

SARAH
And I don't want you to go. But I guess it would be best for your mother. She needs to be with family. And you are smart and brave. I know you'll be all right. You'll see.

HENRY CLAY
I wish I could stay here with you.

JENNY
I wish you could, too.

SARAH
Don't worry, Henry Clay. Things have a way of working out. You don't always know how they're going to work out, but they do.

(SARAH and HENRY CLAY exit upstairs, HENRY CLAY carrying the tray.)

JENNY
He and his mother have to leave next week.

KEENE
He will miss you very much.

JENNY
Yes, and I'll miss him. Would you like more coffee?

KEENE

No, thank you, chéri.

JENNY

I'll light the fire.
>(SHE crosses to the fireplace and lights the fire.)

It's all ready.... There.
>(SHE stands away from the fireplace, and BOTH look into the brightening fire for a moment.)

Do you see pictures in the firelight?

KEENE

Yes. Over there, to the left—a building is burning.

JENNY

It looks like a castle. See, there's the drawbridge. It just fell. It's a war, and everything is burning. Now the people are trapped inside.

KEENE

Or outside. See that lake of fire.

JENNY

It's a moat. Do you think they'll make it safely across?

KEENE

Some of them will.

JENNY

Are the pictures in the fire or in our mind?

KEENE

Either way, they're in our mind.

JENNY

Perhaps you are in my mind, and I am in your mind. And otherwise we aren't real at all.

KEENE
I wouldn't be surprised.

JENNY
Am I in your mind? I mean when you aren't here...? You know, like does a tree falling in a forest make a sound, if no one hears it fall?

KEENE
The truth is—you are in my mind.

JENNY
What am I, in your mind—when you're not here?

KEENE
You are spring—the blossom ready to open—eager and unafraid because you don't know what life is really like. When I think of you, I think of a line from Faust, "Stay, thou art so fair."

JENNY
What does it mean?

KEENE
That this moment is all we have, and it goes too quickly. Hold out your hand to touch it, and it's gone.

JENNY
Gone?

KEENE
Yes, everything goes, too quickly. We are like Faust, you know, wanting what we can't have, crying to the moment, "Stay, thou art so fair."

JENNY
"Stay, thou art so fair."
(THEY look into the fire.)
Look, there's a whole city burning.

KEENE
Yes—Paris, London—all the cities—burning.

JENNY
I can't imagine all those people dying, while everything goes on here as it always has. The war seems so far away—not real.

KEENE
For the young soldiers at Darnell Hospital, war has been much too real.

JENNY
Were they wounded? Is that what drove them crazy?

KEENE
Their wounds are all inside. War makes them do what they've been taught all their lives is wrong.... Suddenly, they have to kill or be killed.... They see their comrades destroyed by a bullet which cares nothing for youth or beauty.... The stress is suddenly—too much. Something breaks inside.

JENNY
The Nazis have done terrible things. Do you think they will go to hell?

KEENE
I think they have made their own hell here on earth.

JENNY
When I was twelve years old, I went to a revival meeting, and they were preaching about the Jews killing Christ, and that's why no Jews are going to heaven.... That would mean my mother is going to hell! Why, I can't imagine wanting to be in heaven and my mother in hell! That would be the worst hell I could think of! Not to be with someone you love!

KEENE
Not to be with someone you love.... Jenny, there's something I have to tell you.

(SARAH and HENRY CLAY enter from upstairs.
Henry Clay is carrying a small box.)

SARAH
Jenny, haven't you changed yet? You better go on upstairs.

JENNY
Mother! Sgt. Keene was just going to tell me....

KEENE
It's all right. I'll tell you later. Better mind your mother.... Think I'll just go out for a smoke.

SARAH
Just relax in the porch swing. I don't know why—but if you just swing back and forth, it takes your mind off your troubles.

(KEENE exits UL.)

HENRY CLAY
(To JENNY.)
Aunt Eula is going to come next week, and take us home with her.

JENNY
I know.

HENRY CLAY
I don't want to go.

JENNY
I know.

SARAH
We don't any of us want you to go, Henry Clay. We'll all miss you. But things will work out, you'll see.... You and your mother will come back to visit us.

(SARAH hugs and kisses HENRY CLAY, then exits into the kitchen UR.)

HENRY CLAY
(Holding out the box to JENNY.)
This is for you.

JENNY
That's your rock collection.

HENRY CLAY
I know.

JENNY
Don't you want it anymore?

HENRY CLAY
No, I don't want to have it. We collected it together.

JENNY
(Taking the box.)
Thank you, Henry Clay.

HENRY CLAY
We won't come back, Jenny, not even for a visit—and my father won't come home.

JENNY
I know. I'll keep this—in my room.

HENRY CLAY
Jenny...Jenny, will you—wait for me 'til I grow up? It won't be long!

JENNY
Oh, Henry Clay—I can't wait for you, and you can't wait for me.... But I'll never forget you. Never! I promise!

(JENNY crosses her heart, and after a painful moment HENRY CLAY responds by crossing his heart. He then exits at the French doors UL. Holding the box of rocks to her heart, JENNY exits up the stairs. FATHER McGREW, carrying several books, enters the "porch" DR, and knocks on the unseen "front door".)

SARAH
(Entering from the kitchen UR and moving downstage, then "opening" the unseen "front door" DR.)
Coming...! Why, you must be the chaplain from out at Darnell Hospital. Do come in.

McGREW
(Entering and crossing DC.)
I am one of the chaplains—Father McGrew.

SARAH
(Also crossing DC.)
I'm Sarah Robinson. It's so nice of you to come by, Father McGrew.

McGREW
Sgt. Myers said it was in the nature of an emergency. I came as quickly as I could.
(HE takes SARAH'S hand.)
May I offer my sincere sympathy?

SARAH
Well, isn't that nice of you? I was feeling bad about it, but we just have to accept these things.

McGREW
That is very brave of you. Is your young man in—very bad shape?

SARAH
Tom? Oh, I wouldn't say that. He is rather anxious.

McGREW
I want you to know that I am prepared to administer the last rites.

SARAH
I certainly hope so. There's so much divorce these days. I think it's the war.

McGREW
Divorce...? The war...? Yes. Well, perhaps I should go up and see him while there's still time.

SARAH
Oh, he's back in the kitchen bottling the rest of that Elixir, and stacking it on the back porch. But you needn't worry. He'll be finished in no time.

McGREW
Finished? Oh, my! And he's still on his feet?

SARAH
Well, I was trying to get him out of the way. I thought it would occupy his mind while he's waiting.

McGREW
Is there any chance he'll survive?

SARAH
Oh, I imagine marriage will cure what ails him.

McGREW
Marriage?!

SARAH
Yes, the wedding. Tom is marrying my daughter, May Anne.

McGREW
I am genuinely touched. A young couple marrying before he goes to the great beyond.

SARAH

He is going overseas any day now.

McGREW

Overseas? In his condition?

SARAH

Well, I imagine his condition will be cured before he leaves.

McGREW

Mrs. Robinson, I came here under the assumption that a patient was dying, and was in need of my services.

SARAH

Oh, my! No! I thought you were acting kind of strange. I was beginning to wonder about you—you being from out there at Darnell, and all.... Oh, no—my daughter May Anne is going to marry a corporal stationed out at Darnell—Tom Young. And we want you to perform the ceremony.

McGREW

Oh, I see! Then you are the proud mother of the happy bride? Congratulations! And where is the proud father?

SARAH

Her father? I'm not sure where he is.

McGREW

Forgive me, I don't mean to pry, but I have heard a great many confessions. In fact, you would not believe the sort of things people confess....

SARAH

I know what you mean. People tell me the strangest things!

McGREW

Do they? Sometimes I don't know what to do or say. Sometimes, I must confess, I feel inadequate.

SARAH

Well, just do the best you can. That's all anyone can do.

McGREW

I know it's hard to believe, but I'm not as wise as I seem. People expect me to have all the answers, but in these perilous times, I'm not sure I'm—up to my calling.

SARAH

I think we all feel that way at times.

McGREW

Do you, Mrs. Robinson?

SARAH

(Patting HIS hand.)
Why, of course. All people really want is someone to listen. Just that makes them feel so much better.

McGREW

I expect you're right.... I want you to know you can confide in me.

SARAH

I'm so glad.

McGREW

Now, about the natural father. Where did this—episode in your life occur? I mean, where did you meet the father of your child?

SARAH

It was almost twenty-two years ago, in Miami Beach.

McGREW

These motel beach resorts....
(HE shrugs helplessly.)
It was just a passing fancy, I suppose.

SARAH

We only knew each other three weeks.

McGREW

And this child was the fruit of that misadventure?

SARAH

I never thought of it that way before—but I see what you mean.... Of course, there were three fruits.

McGREW

Three fruits...! Miss Robinson! Three children out of wedlock?

SARAH

Out of wedlock? Why, wherever did you get that idea...? May I ask you a question, Father?

McGREW

Of course. That's what I'm here for.

SARAH

You seem just a bit, ah.... Were you ever a patient out at the mental hospital?

McGREW

Oh, my, no. I think we've had just a bit of a misunderstanding here. There is a Mr. Robinson?

SARAH

Why, of course.

McGREW

And he is the father of the bride?

SARAH

Yes, but he doesn't know that.

McGREW

But surely Mr. Robinson should know—that he is the father of your children!

SARAH

Oh, he knows my children are his—but he doesn't know that one of them is about to get married.

McGREW

Oh, my! Is that all...? Well, why don't we just share the happy news—now?

SARAH

Have you ever tried sharing happy news with Mr. Robinson...? Anyway, he's not home.

McGREW

Off to the wars, is he?

SARAH

That is a good way to size it up. But he'll be stopping in.

McGREW

I, ah—stopping in?

SARAH

He has his house, and I have mine. It's what seems to work out best for all concerned.

McGREW

Ah! Then—you're separated. I'm pleased that you acknowledge that your church does not condone divorce for practicing Catholics.

SARAH

Why, I didn't know my church would care whether Catholics divorced or not.

McGREW

Mrs. Robinson, you are a Catholic, aren't you?

SARAH

Oh, my, no. Where did you get that idea? I'm Jewish.

McGREW

Then—Mr. Robinson is a Catholic?

SARAH

Oh, no. He hasn't set foot in a church in the twenty-two years I've known him. He's never told us what he is, but he does keep mentioning God Almighty.

McGREW

And—your children?

SARAH

Well, they used to be Southern Baptists like their father's people. But Andrew joined the Navy and became an Ensign, and May Anne went over to the Episcopal Church with her best friend, until they converted to tennis lessons. Jenny says she's an atheist—but I told her she'd outgrow it.

McGREW

Oh, my. Oh, my.... And—the groom?

SARAH

I think he's a Unitarian.

McGREW

A Unitarian! Oh, my God! I think there's something you should know, Mrs. Robinson! I am a Roman Catholic Priest!

SARAH

Well, isn't that nice? I think everyone should believe in something.

McGREW

But you don't understand! I cannot marry someone who is not a Catholic!

SARAH

Why, Father, are you thinking of getting married, too? Well, I'm sure you'll find a nice Catholic girl, from a very nice family.

McGREW

Mrs. Robinson! Catholic Priests perform marriage ceremonies for others—for couples who are Catholic...! I, ah, don't know who would marry a Unitarian!

SARAH

Oh, so you are a chaplain for just Catholics?

McGREW

On the battlefield, Mrs. Robinson, God does not check credentials. If a boy is dying, it doesn't matter whether he is Catholic, Protestant, or Jewish. I am prepared to offer him my services. These books contain everything I need to know.

SARAH

Everything?

McGREW

Everything. For example, I can confess a French soldier, even though I speak no French. It's done by the numbers. You see, I point to Question Nine: Have you committed carnal sin? The soldier reads Question Nine in his language, and shakes his head, Yes. I point to Question Ten: How many times? The soldier reads Question Ten in his language, and holds up his fingers. Five, ten, fifteen, seventeen, whatever, times. Then I absolve him in Latin, which neither of us understands. Beats all the older forms of Confession, to my way of thinking. Something we should stay with, after the war.

SARAH
But it's not just Confession you have in all those books.... You have—everything.

McGREW
Everything. From the cradle to the grave!

SARAH
And you thought Tom was dying, so you came here with your books all set to bury him...? Well, getting him married is just about the same thing, so—we can just go right ahead.

McGREW
Mrs. Robinson, my guide books cover almost any eventuality, but I cannot believe they include a ceremony that would unite tennis lessons with a Unitarian.

SARAH
Then we'll just have to make it up as we go along. Tom wants to keep it short, anyhow. He only has a three-day pass.

McGREW
But Mrs. Robinson! You don't understand....

SARAH
Father McGrew, you are prepared for emergencies, aren't you?

McGREW
Yes, I am. But....

SARAH
Father! This is in the nature of an emergency!

McGREW
(Wary.)
An—emergency?

SARAH
If you know what I mean...! You do know what I mean?

McGREW
(A slow take.)
Oh, my.... Oh, my...! I—see! Well, in that case....

SARAH
And Cpl. Young is one of your own boys, and he's going overseas, leaving May Anne when she's...you do understand?

McGREW
I do, indeed.

SARAH
I'm so glad we got that settled. I'll just call everyone.

McGREW
But, Mrs. Robinson....

TOM
(Entering from the kitchen UR, carrying a bottle of Elixir, and not immediately reacting to McGREW'S presence.)
Miz Robinson, Jeff wants to see you in the kitchen about this Elixir.

SARAH
In a minute, Tom.

TOM
But Jeff said....

SARAH
Father, this is Cpl. Tom Young. Tom, this is Father McGrew.

TOM
(A slow take, then overjoyed.)
I'm so glad you're here, Father. You don't know how worried I've been!

McGREW
I do. I do, indeed, Corporal. Mrs. Robinson has—explained. Now, about the ceremony....

SARAH
Come into the kitchen with me, Father. While we're talking about the ceremony you can have a sip of that Elixir. It'll do you a world of good.
(Calling upstairs.)
May Anne! Jenny! Sgt. Keene! The Chaplain is here! It's time for the wedding! Henry Clay, tell your mother you're both invited!

(SARAH, TOM and McGREW exit into the kitchen. KEENE enters UL. JENNY starts down the stairs. KEENE stands observing Jenny's descent. JENNY is wearing a very becoming Princess style dress with high heels, and her hair is up in a more mature style. She seems almost grown up. SHE stops to pose on the stairs, aware of how pretty she is. KEENE looks at her as though he has never seen her before.)

KEENE
Don't move—for a moment. "Stay, thou art so fair."
(HE takes a single flower from the vase and hands it to HER.)
When I am far away, I will remember how beautiful you are at this moment.

JENNY
Far away?

KEENE
Yes, there's something I have to tell you.

JENNY
You're leaving, too, aren't you?

KEENE
I'm being transferred.

JENNY
Where will they send you?

KEENE
Germany, I'm sure.

JENNY
But you said the war with Germany was almost over.

KEENE
It is, but they'll need translators during the Occupation.

JENNY
When will you be going?

KEENE
Next week.

JENNY
Next week! But that's so soon! How can they make you go so soon?

KEENE
They can make us do whatever they want. That's the way it is.

JENNY
But nothing will be the same if you go.

KEENE
Everything changes.

JENNY
May Anne is going to marry Tom, Andrew is gone, Henry Clay is leaving, and now you're leaving, too! Nothing will be all right if you leave! Oh—please don't go!

KEENE
I don't have any choice. Chéri, you do what you have to do, and you do it as well as you know how. That's all that counts. I won't forget you, Jenny—or your mother—and your kindness to me.

JENNY
I will never forget you! Never! As long as I live!

KEENE
And I will never forget you—and the way you look tonight.

(Very gently, HE kisses HER hand.)

JENNY
Sgt. Keene—there's….there's something I want to tell you before you go.

(JENNY becomes silent when she sees HENRY CLAY at the French doors. Clearly, he has been eavesdropping. He enters glumly as SARAH and McGREW enter from the kitchen UR. McGREW is carrying a bottle of Sarah's Elixir. TOM enters from the kitchen through the dining room UC just in time to see MAY ANNE enter, descending the stairs. MAY ANNE wears a white Princess style dress with pink ribbon bows at the shoulders, a pink ribbon sash, and white high heels.)

TOM
You're the most beautiful bride in the world!

SARAH
Oh, how beautiful you look! Both of you are so beautiful!
> (SHE hugs JENNY and MAY ANNE.)

You need some flowers.
> (SARAH takes the bouquet from the hall table vase and hands it to MAY ANNE.)

There. Father McGrew, this is my daughter, May Anne, and my daughter, Jenny. And this is Sgt. Keene and Henry Clay.

> (MAY ANNE, JENNY, and HENRY CLAY greet McGREW silently.)

KEENE
Good of you to come, Father.

> (McGREW acknowledges the OTHERS, shakes hands with KEENE, then crosses to the fireplace DL.)

MAY ANNE
Mother, what about Daddy?

SARAH
I don't think we better wait for your father. We'll just—surprise him.
> (SARAH sings as she positions MAY ANNE and TOM before McGREW.)

Here comes the bride!
Here comes the bride!
Here comes the bride
With the groom at her side!

MAY ANNE
(To JENNY.)
Stand here by me! You're my maid of honor!

TOM
And—will you be my Best Man, Sgt. Keene?

KEENE
I would be honored.

(JENNY stands beside MAY ANNE, and KEENE stands beside TOM. McGREW, the while, is searching through his books.)

MAY ANNE
Oh, Tom! We don't have a ring!

TOM
A—ring?

SARAH
Yes, you do! Here, Henry Clay....
(SARAH removes her own ring and hands it to HENRY CLAY.)
you can be the ring bearer.
(To MAY ANNE and TOM.)
I hope you two will be just as happy as we've been.

MAY ANNE
Oh, how romantic.

McGREW
(Continuing a forlorn search through HIS books.)
These books don't even mention Unitarians!

SARAH
Don't worry about it, Father. Whatever comes to mind will do just fine. We don't have much time.

                          McGREW
            (After another hurried sip of the Elixir. Then, HE
            speaks in deeply officious tones.)
Dearly beloved, we are gathered here in the sight of God to unite
this couple in the bonds of holy matrimony.... TOM, do you take
Mary Anne....

                          SARAH
May Anne.

                          McGREW
...for your lawful wedded wife, for richer or for poorer, in sickness
or in health....
            (McGREW forgets what comes next.)

                          SARAH
For better or for worse.

                          McGREW
For better or for worse, so long as ye both shall live?

                           TOM
I do.

            (Prompted by a nod from SARAH, HENRY CLAY
            gives the ring to TOM, who slips the ring onto MAY
            ANNE'S finger.)

                          McGREW
Mary Anne...

                         MAY ANNE
May Anne!

                          McGREW
...do you take Tom for your lawful wedded husband, for richer or
for poorer, in sickness or in health, for better or for worse....

JEFF
(Entering hurriedly UR, interrupting.)
Miz Robinson, you better come out here! Way that there Elixir's actin'....

SARAH
Not now, Jeff! We've got a wedding going on! You and Aunt Martha just leave that Elixir alone, and come on in here!

JEFF
That there Elixir ain't goin' to let us study no wedding!

MAY ANNE
(Stamping HER foot and yelling shrilly.)
Mother! This is my wedding!

SARAH
Not now, Jeff! I'll be there in a minute!

JEFF
(Exiting UR.)
Well, don't blame me.

SARAH
Now, where were we? Oh, yes, you were saying....

McGREW
(After another quick sip of the Elixir.)
Dearly beloved....

SARAH
Just skip on over to "for better or worse." That's the main part, anyhow.

McGREW
Mary Anne....

SARAH and MAY ANNE

May Anne!

McGREW

...do you take Tom for your lawful wedded husband, et cetera, et cetera, and for better or for worse, so long as ye both shall live?

MAY ANNE

I do.

McGREW

If there is anyone who can show just cause why these two should not be united in holy matrimony, let him speak now or forever hold his peace.

(SOUND of pots and pans clattering OFF L.)

EVAN
(From OFF L.)

Sarah!

(EVAN enters through the French doors UL. He is carrying the strung-together pots and pans.)

Sarah!

(HE stares at the gathering in astonishment.)

McGREW
(Most tentatively.)
So this is the happy father of the bride?

EVAN
(Struggling to understand.)

Bride?

(Understanding.)

Bride?!!

(EVAN hurls the pots and pans out the French doors UL.)

McGREW

Oh, my!

(Racing the words.)

I now pronounce you man and wife. Kiss the bride. Congratulations to all!

(Clutching his books and his bottle, McGREW tries to escape out the "front door" DR.)

EVAN

(Hurriedly crossing to intercept McGREW.)

Now just a minute! What do you think you're doing here?

McGREW

I don't think I can explain it.

(McGREW retreats to the foot of the stairs DR, where he stands staring in disbelief at the goings-on—taking further swigs of the Elixir.)

EVAN

Sarah! This is all your fault!

SARAH

I thought it would be.

(The repeated sips of the Elixir are having a beneficial effect on McGREW. Sarah's Elixir works. McGREW is feeling no pain.)

EVAN

(To MAY ANNE.)

Why in the name of God didn't you tell me you were getting married?

MAY ANNE

Because you always yell.

EVAN

(Yelling.)

I always yell?!

MAY ANNE

Like you're doing now—and I didn't want to upset you. Because I love you, Daddy—and I want you to be happy.... Daddy, you want me to be happy, don't you?

EVAN

Happy! You don't know what you're getting into...! You're both so young!

MAY ANNE

Momma is always talking about how you two were young and in love under that Miami moon.

EVAN

What's that Miami moon got to do with you getting married?

MAY ANNE

Daddy! Don't you understand? This is our Kentucky moon!

EVAN

Your Kentucky moon!

MAY ANNE

I've heard of your Miami moon all my life! Daddy, this is our Kentucky moon—and it's right now!

SARAH

Evan, don't you remember what it was like being young and in love? How we used to walk on the beach night after night under that madcap moon, just happy to be together.

EVAN
Under that madcap moon.

SARAH
(Softly.)
Evan...you do remember.

EVAN
Remember...? Sarah, here we are, still together. I guess that means— I remember.

>(For a moment, SARAH and EVAN are alone together under that Miami moon.)

MAY ANNE
Oh, Daddy, won't you wish us happiness?
>(EVAN hesitates, then, finding it ever so difficult, he draws MAY ANNE into an unaccustomed, awkward embrace. SHE kisses EVAN.)

Oh, Daddy, thank you!

>(EVAN hesitates again, then offers his hand to TOM. They shake hands.)

SARAH
It's time to toss that bridal bouquet!

>(Taking note of JENNY'S location, MAY ANNE turns her back, and takes aim.)

EVAN
(Spontaneously, to JENNY.)
Don't catch it!

>(Facing away from JENNY, MAY ANNE tosses the bouquet backward, over her head. JENNY catches it.)

SARAH
(Beaming.)
Father, what do we owe you for the wedding?

McGREW
(Evidencing mild intoxication.)
Mrs. Robinson, you have a gold mine in this Elixir. If you could just spare a few bottles....

EVAN
Sarah! What did I tell you about that Elixir?

(JEFF enters in a rush from the kitchen UR.)

JEFF
Miz Robinson! Miz Robinson! It's—it's the war! The war! It's over! That there radio....
(HE is pointing to the kitchen UR.)
...just said Berlin fell!

EVAN
Berlin fell?!

(HE quickly turns on the living room radio. ALL listen intently.)

VOICE ON RADIO
(A continuation of an announcement in progress.)
...this afternoon, at the end of twelve days of history's deadliest street fighting. Seventy thousand German troops laid down their arms in the surrender that Adolf Hitler said would never come. At the end of one of the bloodiest struggles known to mankind, the war in Europe is over.

(Period MUSIC is heard following the announcement, the MUSIC continuing softly under what follows.)

                          EVAN
It's over!

                          SARAH
Oh, thank God!

              (TOM slaps HENRY CLAY on the back, and they
              both emit a war whoop.)

                          MAY ANNE
It's over!

              (MAY ANNE and JENNY hug.)

                          TOM
It's really over!

              (TOM hugs MAY ANNE, as SARAH, HENRY
              CLAY, and JENNY hug each other.)

                          JEFF
That there war shor is over!

              (JEFF and EVAN shake hands.)

                          MAY ANNE
Oh, Daddy!

              (MAY ANNE kisses and hugs EVAN.)

                          TOM
Sergeant!

              (TOM shakes hands with KEENE, then both TOM
              and KEENE shake McGREW'S hand, and both
              shake JEFF'S hand.)

EVAN
Sarah, the war in Europe is over.

SARAH
Oh, Evan, soon it will all be over, and Andrew will be coming home! We'll all be together again!

> (SARAH and EVAN hug each other. SOUND of an explosion, OFF UR. In a panic, JEFF exits into the kitchen UR.)

SARAH
Oh, no!

EVAN
Sarah! What is going on out there?

JEFF
> (Reentering from the kitchen UR.)

Miz Robinson! That Elixir done exploded all over the back porch!

> (JEFF hurriedly exits into the kitchen UR.)

EVAN
> (As HE follows JEFF, exiting UR.)

Sarah, you will be the death of me yet!

SARAH
> (Also exiting UR.)

It's the war, I guess.

HENRY CLAY
> (As HE exits UR.)

I'm going to miss this place!

McGREW
May the peace of the Lord be with you all!

(McGREW staggers off, exiting DR, books and bottle in hand.)

TOM

Oh, May Anne, I only had a three-day pass, and now there are only two days left!

MAY ANNE

Yes, Tom. Only two days—but three nights!

(SHE grabs TOM, and pulls him up the stairs.)

KEENE

(To JENNY.)

Your family will want to be together. I'll just—slip away. Tell your mother I wish all of you happiness and love.

JENNY

(Still holding the bridal bouquet.)

Sgt. Keene, will you—will you wait for me 'til I grow up?

KEENE

(Reaching out to tilt HER chin so that HE can look into her eyes.)

Chéri—you won't wait for me.

(HE gently kisses HER hand, in the Continental manner then quickly exits DR. JENNY stands, clutching her bouquet, looking after him. Perhaps she raises her arm—not as a wave, but as a gesture of longing, and of good-bye.)

SLOW FADE to BLACK.

END of the PLAY

APPENDIX

THAT MADCAP MOON
PRODUCTIONS, WORKSHOPS, READINGS, AND AWARDS AND HONORS

Productions
2011 Pioneer Playhouse, Danville, Kentucky
2011 Black Bart Players, Murphys, California
1999 Mississippi State University, Mississippi
1999 Spotlight Theatre, Bulverde, Texas
1999 Pioneer Playhouse, Danville, Kentucky
1999 Westside Players, Pocatello, Idaho
1998 Henrico Theatre Company, Richmond, Virginia
1995 Sheboygan Theatre Company, Sheboygan, Wisconsin
1992 Georgia Repertory Theatre, Athens, Georgia *(Equity mainstage production)*
1991 Theatre Americana, Altadena, California
1988 Baldwin Theatre, Royal Oak, Michigan

Staged Readings and Readings
1989 Southern Appalachian Playwrights' Conference, Mars Hill, North Carolina
1988 WPA Theatre (Off Broadway), New York City *(staged reading)*

Awards and Honors
1992 Winner of a National Broadcasting Company "New Voices" Program Grant supporting a residency at Georgia Repertory Theatre, Athens, Georgia
1991 Finalist, Colonial Players, Annapolis, Maryland
1990 Winner in Theatre Americana's National Playwriting Competition, Altadena, California

1990 Finalist, Elmira College Competition, New York

1989 Chosen for Southern Appalachian Playwrights' Conference, Mars Hill, North Carolina

1988 Chosen for WPA Theatre (Off Broadway) Phase I Series, New York City, New York (under earlier title, *The Follies of '45*)

1987 Finalist, National Playwrights' Conference, O'Neill Center, Connecticut

1986 One of four finalists, Honorable Mention, Southeastern Theatre New Play Project

1986 Finalist, Dalton Theatre Contest

1985 Finalist, National Repertory Theatre Foundation National Award, Los Angeles, California

ABOUT THE AUTHORS

Jan Henson Dow has won more than 150 national playwriting competitions, awards, and honors, including an NBC New Voices Award. Her plays have received numerous productions, workshops, and staged readings around the country, and her full-length plays have been published by Samuel French, Popular Play Service, and Phosphene Publishing Company.

As a professor at Western Connecticut State University, Dow directed the Playwriting Workshops and co-produced Western's Festival of New Plays. She has been the recipient of a number of playwriting grants, as well as grants for the new play festivals. She also taught playwriting workshops at the Osher Life Long Learning Institute at the University of South Carolina and at workshops around the country. Her articles and poems have appeared in such publications as *The New York Times*, *The Dramatists Guild Quarterly*, *Kansas Quarterly*, and *Indiana Review*. She co-authored *Writing the Award Winning Play* with Shannon Michal Dow, and they have just completed their first novel, *The Darkest Lies*. Jan is a member of the Dramatists Guild.

Robert Schroeder won a number of playwriting competitions, including an NBC New Voices Award. His plays have been staged nationally. He served on the staff of *The Dramatist Guild Quarterly* and the Dodd-Mead *Best Plays* reference annuals. His reviews and theatre commentaries also appeared in *The Nation, Commonweal, New York*, and other periodicals. His anthology, *The New Underground Theatre*, was published by Bantam Books, and he was among the contributors to *Playwrights, Lyricists, and Composers on Theatre*, a Dodd-Mead hardcover. He was often retained professionally as a play/musical "doctor" for a number of Off Broadway productions.

Phosphene Publishing Company publishes books and DVDs relating to literature, history, the paranormal, film, spirituality, and the martial arts.

For other great titles, visit
phosphenepublishing.com

www.ingramcontent.com/pod-product-compliance
Lightning Source LLC
Chambersburg PA
CBHW061943070426
42450CB00007BA/1041